# Are You an Indigo Adult?

## A Guide for Sensitive Souls Seeking Transformation and Meaning

STEFANO PRATT

Copyright © 2024 Stefano Pratt

All rights reserved. No part of this book may be reproduced, stored in a retrieval system, or transmitted in any form or by any means—electronic, mechanical, photocopying, recording, or otherwise—without the prior written permission of the author or publisher. Unauthorized duplication, distribution, or partial use of this material is strictly prohibited and may result in legal action.

ISBN: 9798306427621

**To my mother,**

who taught me to love life, even in its silences,

who planted in me the courage to dream and the strength to rise again.

Your light continues to shine with every step I take,

and your love is the invisible thread that ties my days together.

This book is a tribute to your memory,

an eternal embrace between heaven and earth.

Are You an Indigo Adult?

Dear Reader,

Thank you for choosing this book. It is no coincidence that you find yourself here, in this moment, holding these pages in your hands. Perhaps you are seeking answers, a new perspective, or a deeper connection with yourself and the world around you.

My goal in writing this book is to guide you on this journey. As an author, explorer of inner worlds, and passionate seeker of spirituality, my mission is to offer you tools, reflections, and inspiration to help uncover your true essence and life purpose.

Together, we will delve into the subtle energies that animate your being, the profound connections that weave our lives together, and the paths of meaning that link your inner world to the infinite universe around you.

Join me on this unique adventure and let this book become your compass, guiding you to discover your true self, transform your sensitivity into strength, and fully embrace your inner light.

With gratitude,
Stefano Pratt

|  | | |
|---|---|---|
|  | Introduction | 1 |
| 1 | The Beginning Of A Journey | 5 |
| 2 | Following The Signs Means Finding The Right Path | 11 |
| 3 | What Is An Indigo Adult? | 18 |
| 4 | The Traits That Confirm You Are An Indigo Adult | 25 |
| 5 | The Second Test: Are You An Indigo Adult? | 39 |
| 6 | Third Test To Better Understand Your Indigo Identity | 44 |
| 7 | Voices That Remind You Are Not Alone | 49 |
| 8 | Synchronicity: The Spiritual Navigation System Of The Indigo Souls | 83 |
| 9 | Indigo Children: Embracing The Wisdom Of Sensitive Souls | 93 |
| 10 | The Mission Of The Indigos On Earth | 102 |
| 11 | How To Break Free From Our Prison | 110 |
| 12 | Indigo Adults And The Politics Of Our Time | 118 |
| 13 | The Dark Night Of The Soul: What To Do When Everything Goes Wrong? | 123 |
| 14 | How To Stop Absorbing Other People's Emotions | 132 |
| 15 | How To Develop Your Psychic And Spiritual Abilities (Without Fear) | 147 |
| 16 | Indigo Relationships: Building Deep And Authentic Connections | 154 |
| 17 | The Toxic Relationship Between Indigo Adults And Narcissistic Manipulators | 160 |
| 18 | Indigo Adults: Balancing A Traditional Career And Authentic Personal Fulfillment | 164 |
| 19 | How to Help an Indigo Adult | 177 |
|  | Conclusion | 180 |
|  | About the Author | 184 |

**Acknowledgments**

To all the people who believed in me,

thank you for your trust, your support, and your unwavering faith in my projects, even when my ideas seemed to stray far from the beaten path.
To Fabienne, whose encouragement has been a guiding light in moments of doubt. Your support gave wings to my dreams and allowed me to complete this adventure.
To my brother Simone, a loyal accomplice who has always welcomed my ideas—no matter how unconventional—with kindness and humor. Thank you for being there, with your open heart and reassuring presence, reminding me that originality is a strength.
Each of you, in your own way, is an essential part of this book.
I did not walk this path alone.
Thank you for everything.

# INTRODUCTION

*"We are not human beings having a spiritual experience. We are spiritual beings having a human experience"*. – Teilhard de Chardin

**Thank You for Being Here**

Thank you for choosing to embark on this journey of personal growth. Each page you turn is a step toward greater awareness and a deeper love for yourself and others. I want to express my heartfelt gratitude for your presence and commitment to this adventure. By choosing to read this book, you have already taken a significant step toward a more enlightened and fulfilling life.

Every word written here is meant to inspire you, to awaken a sense of self-awareness and love within you that can illuminate every aspect of your existence. This book has been crafted for readers to discover more about themselves simply by reading it from start to finish.

Throughout its chapters, you'll find stories—both my own and those of others—that illustrate our shared journeys toward self-realization. These stories aim to guide and inspire you, connecting to your personal experiences and echoing your own path. I have done the work for you: all you need to do is read, absorb, and reflect.

As you explore this book, you will also uncover a new vision of the world. This vision is filled with hope and infinite possibilities. It invites you to participate in creating a new world—one where compassion, empathy, and collective consciousness are at the heart of our actions.

This journey has profoundly transformed and enriched me. It has brought me clarity and inner peace I never knew before. I sincerely hope it will do the same for you. By sharing my experiences and insights, my wish is to inspire you to embrace your own path of growth and transformation.

I encourage you to share your discoveries with others, to build a community of light and support. Together, we can elevate collective consciousness and create a more harmonious and compassionate world. Your contribution is valuable and has a meaningful impact.

**What is an Indigo?**

I'll discuss this in detail throughout the book and, more importantly, provide you with tools to determine whether you might be an "Indigo."

For now, I can tell you that these individuals often feel ahead of their time, frequently struggle to find their place in society, and sometimes feel alone.

**Does this sound familiar?**

Read this book, and you'll discover a new dimension of yourself. Many people are entirely unaware of this reality. If the contents of this book have reached your consciousness, it's either because you're curious and likely need the information it contains to continue your evolution, because you are yourself an Indigo, or because you live surrounded by Indigos and feel an urgent need to understand what this means.

The presence of this phenomenon—people with high potential and a developed spirituality—is not a coincidence. This is not a religious movement, a cult, or a mere fantasy of enlightened dreamers. It is a reality. Across the globe, there are individuals—both children and adults—capable of things that go beyond common understanding.

In this book, I will share the knowledge I have gathered on this topic. My goal is to pave the way toward a deeper understanding of our true nature and the fulfillment of our highest potential.

This book is the result of an adventure spanning more than ten years, which began as a blog dedicated to this very topic. Over time, that blog became a gathering place for thoughts, comments, and experiences from passionate readers. The pages you are about to read are therefore not only based on my personal reflections and experiences but also enriched by the daily realities and stories of thousands of people who have recognized Indigo traits within themselves and their lives.

Some of these reflections and fragments of wisdom shared by readers have left an indelible mark and found a special place within this book. Wherever their relevance aligns with collective wisdom, I have integrated them into these pages, considering them precious gems worthy of being shared with you, just as they were with those who initially contributed and read them.

Even though the blog no longer exists, the essential knowledge and core teachings from that time have been preserved and condensed into these pages. This book is thus much more than a simple continuation; it is the natural, refined evolution of that shared adventure.

This book was written to offer you tools to understand your true nature, discover who you can become, and reconnect with your essence and life mission.

If you feel exhausted, drained, or lost, if time and energy always seem to be in short supply, or if you haven't yet found the path to fully realizing your potential and achieving your deepest aspirations, this book will provide you with the keys to understanding what truly ignites your passion and makes you feel alive. It will guide you to uncover your "life mission".

This book also has a "magical" dimension. You might find yourself compelled to revisit it over time, discovering layers of deeper meaning within its pages. This was the perspective with which it was written. While much of what is said about Indigos specifically applies to them, it is not exclusive to them. In fact, all inhabitants of this planet are beginning to experience extraordinary phenomena, especially those who have taken control of their destiny and realized their deepest aspirations.

These pages are the fruit of my ongoing commitment to bring greater clarity and understanding. Let yourself be guided by the words and stories, allowing this book to lead you toward an awakening of consciousness that will reveal aspects of yourself you may have never explored.

Imagine yourself walking a path illuminated by your inner light, a journey leading you to realize your highest potential. Each step you take is an act of love toward yourself, a way to honor your uniqueness and strength.

This book is your travel companion, a guide to support, inspire, and remind you every day how extraordinary you are. As you read, you'll feel a new energy grow within you—a desire to explore, learn, and evolve.

Whether you are an Indigo adult or not, I invite you to immerse yourself in these pages, allowing every word to touch your heart and awaken that spark of divine beauty within you.

You are at the center of this transformation. It will be your open mind and willingness to grow that will bring this journey to life. Take each teaching to heart, apply it to your daily life, and watch the miracles unfold.

The awakening of consciousness is a powerful phenomenon, a true inner awakening that allows you to see the world with fresh eyes. It leads to a deeper understanding of yourself and your place in the universe. It paves the way for personal rebirth—a transformation that guides you to live more authentically, in harmony with your values and highest aspirations.

This book doesn't aim to provide "ready-made" answers. Instead, it's here to remind you of what you already know deep within yourself. It encourages you to explore, dream, and reconnect with that infinite source of wisdom and joy residing inside you.

Keep this book as your travel companion. Let its words guide you, but above all, listen to your heart. For it is there, in the silence of your soul, that you will find the most precious answers. The journey is just beginning, and I am honored to walk it with you, every step of the way.

# 1 THE BEGINNING OF A JOURNEY

*"What lies behind us and what lies ahead of us are tiny matters compared to what lies within us"*. – Ralph Waldo Emerson

*"The greatest of illusions is believing that our world is limited"*. – Carlos Castaneda

*"It is not the world that is too small; it is our perspective that is too narrow"*. – Paul Éluard

For the first time, I began to truly notice the splendor all around me, as if something within me had shifted, opening my eyes to the beauty that had always been there. A gentle spring breeze softly touched my face, carrying with it a feeling of renewal and calm, while a golden light seemed to flow effortlessly over every corner of this city, so alive with history and beauty. It felt as though that light wasn't just around me but also entering me, filling my eyes and warming my heart, leaving behind a profound, unshakable sense of comfort and belonging. I walked aimlessly toward Largo di Torre Argentina in Rome.

What I love most about this city is losing myself in its streets and squares, discovering hidden and unexpected corners. Largo di Torre Argentina is famous as the site where, on the Ides of March in 44 B.C., Julius Caesar was assassinated in one of history's most renowned conspiracies[1]. This site preserves the remains of several ancient temples,

---

[1] It is believed that the name "Argentina" might derive from Argentoratum,

including the Temple of Pompeius, where the assassination took place. The temple, part of the Pompeius Theater complex, embodies the intersection of political and religious power in ancient Rome, a central theme in Roman culture.

Delving into the deep roots of Rome's spiritual heritage, one cannot overlook the legacy of the Etruscans, whose rituals and divination practices were integral to ancient Roman religion. The Etruscans mastered the art of communicating with the divine, interpreting the signs of nature, and performing complex rituals with shamanic elements.

Not far from Rome, in the countryside, lies the mysterious Etruscan Pyramid, a place shrouded in mystery and charged with ancient energy. Although I cannot reveal all the details at this moment, it is said that something very significant happened there—an event that echoes across the ages.

As I reflected on how the stories of people and places are inextricably intertwined, I began to grasp the depth of it all. I felt like a part of this tapestry, as though I was ready to embark on a long journey—a journey not only through space but also through time and the deep connections that link us to what has been and what will be.

For a long time, I blamed others for my unhappiness, having lived a life that didn't feel truly mine. This was evident in my inability to genuinely appreciate anything. My life felt like a movie playing out before me, one I wasn't truly living. My work brought no satisfaction, my relationship offered no enrichment, and even my sense of identity felt distant and unfamiliar.

Until that moment, my life had followed a path I didn't like, for reasons I couldn't understand, and I mistakenly believed I had no alternatives.

*"Who am I really?"*

An intriguing question. I needed to find the answer, and time was running out. A decisive turning point was fast approaching:

***"Should I accept the new professional opportunity abroad and change everything?"***

---

the current city of Strasbourg, birthplace of Johannes Burckardt, master of ceremonies to Pope Alexander VI Borgia, who may have given the name "Argentina" to the tower of his palace. However, the origin of Strasbourg's name is Celtic and likely means "place of the silver river," probably referring to the Ill River that flows through the city.

This name was later Latinized by the Romans, with the root "argentum" symbolizing sparkling or clear water, akin to silver.

At the beginning of my journey of self-discovery, I immersed myself in various perspectives on personal development, initiating a profound paradigm shift in my life. Over time, my dedication to personal growth and spirituality grew, transforming into an exhilarating and transformative inner quest.

During this period of metamorphosis, I was fortunate to encounter guides—people who inspired me and truly changed the course of my life. Their arrival seemed almost coincidental, but their presence was always crucial. These guides appeared at the right moment, offering valuable teachings and illuminating advice that deeply resonated with my inner journey.

Once the journey had begun, it became clear there was no turning back.

Every step, every encounter, every lesson represented another milestone toward inner transformation, marking an irreversible shift in perspective.

I had come to understand that our minds shape our reality—that I was not a victim but the master of my destiny. What I once interpreted as a lack of opportunities transformed into abundance, much like learning a new language that opens doors to new possibilities and enriches our lives.

Sometimes we feel stuck, as I did at the beginning of this journey. However, when we truly begin to search for who we are, opportunities start to flow, making it difficult to discern which path is the right one for us.

As the light faded and the evening crept in with its quiet presence, I felt the need to return home. Walking toward the first bus stop, I sensed questions rising within me, like delicate threads interwoven, akin to the distant notes of a mysterious melody. These questions, almost imperceptibly, demanded my attention, stirring a subtle energy and a quiet electricity.

It felt as if the possibilities before me were far greater than I had ever imagined. I had the impression that my desires were seeking to enter my field of vision, but it was up to me to open the door for them.

The first bus approached slowly, releasing a gentle hiss as it came to a stop. I stepped on board, book in hand, and tried to resume reading. Yet after just a few lines, my focus slipped away entirely.

Then, something unexpected happened: a stranger seated next to me on the bus spoke to me.

*"It seems you're at a crossroads, and a decision is now inevitable, isn't it?"*

At the time, I was naturally reserved, reluctant to open up, and certainly not the kind of person to attract attention, especially from strangers. She was a woman of mysterious beauty, likely in her forties, while I was just twenty-three. She had long dark hair and amber eyes, intense and piercing, radiating a singular energy. Her gaze was sharp yet curious, and her presence exuded an undeniable magnetism.

I shared my situation with her, speaking with the casual ease of someone confiding in a stranger—like narrating a story to someone you're certain you'll never meet again.

At times, I feel enveloped by a sense of protection. Circumstances that appear random may, in reality, hold profound meaning, pointing the way to the next stage of our personal evolution.

I am deeply convinced that for each of us, a path, a journey, and a destiny of growth unfolds, enabling us to develop and explore a positive vision of the future.

Yet, simplicity is often anything but simple. Following one's inspiration requires careful listening; there is a subtle voice that whispers rather than shouts—a faint but constant presence that can only be heard if we choose to pay attention. It's like an undertone of music, resonating while we are immersed in other tasks, occasionally surfacing amidst the folds of our thoughts.

Her gaze locked onto mine, maintaining a silence for a few moments before she spoke words I would reflect on for years to come:

***"Our path holds the fruits we seek; don't let the urge to control everything overwhelm you. Trust your intuition—it is the only truth that can truly guide and inspire you".***

If you are reading these pages, I am certain you have already experienced some of the moments I describe, while others I will share may feel new or difficult to understand. I do not ask you to passively believe in what I say; on the contrary, I invite you to remain vigilant: discover what resonates within you, what you instinctively feel to be true.

In short, take what is useful to you and let go of the rest.
Before continuing, I invite you to try a brief exercise:
Just begin by noticing your breath—there's no need to change it, just notice.

As you gently inhale and exhale, allow a sense of ease to begin flowing through you, as if each breath carries with it a wave of relaxation. You might find that with each breath, a sense of calm naturally arises, or perhaps it feels like a gentle settling within.

You may start to remember a moment in your life—a time when you felt clarity and certainty, almost effortlessly. Perhaps it was a special place, somewhere that felt safe, comforting, and free. Or maybe it's something different, unique to you. Whatever it is, allow it to come into your awareness now, in a way that feels just right for you.

Imagine yourself in that moment. Notice the colors, the sounds, or even the feelings that come with it. And as you breathe, you might begin to sense a growing serenity wrapping around you like a soft, warm embrace.

And as this peacefulness deepens, you may find that your mind naturally begins to relax, opening up to new possibilities. You might even notice that certain doors—doors you hadn't seen before—are quietly waiting for you to recognize them. And you can take all the time you need to notice those doors and what they represent.

Now, imagine these doors gently opening, one by one, revealing opportunities that feel right, like they've been there all along, just waiting for this very moment. You don't need to rush—simply let them reveal themselves in their own time.

As you allow this process to unfold, you may notice a voice within you, soft yet certain, guiding you. This voice, your inner wisdom, knows exactly what you need. It speaks with calm clarity, gently pointing the way forward.

You might realize that every step you take, every choice you make, is an act of love toward yourself. And as you follow this path, the doubts that may have held you back begin to fade, replaced by a quiet confidence and a deep sense of inner peace.

And you can allow yourself to feel that transformation growing within you now—a sense of becoming, a gentle awakening to who you truly are and what you are meant to do.

Take as much time as you need in this space. And as you finish this exercise, you might carry with you a new sense of clarity, trust in your journey, and perhaps even excitement for what lies ahead.

## 2 FOLLOWING THE SIGNS MEANS FINDING THE RIGHT PATH

*"Know yourself, and you will know the universe and the gods"*. – Inscription from the Temple of Delphi, attributed to Socrates

*"The path is made by walking"*. – Antonio Machado

*"Intuition is a spiritual faculty; it cannot be explained but only felt"*. – Florence Scovel Shinn

**Learner:** "Master, I understand that I'm here to learn from you. I want to discover who I truly am and what I must do to find my path".
**Master:** "I have nothing to teach you about yourself. What you will find here are simple tools—fragments that may spark an echo within you, a memory, or perhaps a sense of connection to those deeper realities that are already yours. To remember oneself is like finding the way back to Atlantis".
**Learner:** "Atlantis… a place I thought was lost forever. Is it truly possible to find it again?"
**Master:** "Atlantis is not just a place; it is a state of being—an ancient memory of who we are. Let me tell you a story.
Once, in the depths of space and time, there was an enchanted realm that rose from the waters. The inhabitants of this place possessed extraordinary powers: they shaped matter, communicated across vast distances, and lived in boundless abundance. They knew neither

scarcity nor conflict, for everything was in harmony with the universal laws that connected them to the Whole.

They lived in magical stillness, aware of the balance between nature and emotions, always seeking harmony in their relationships with themselves, with others, and with the world around them. Even death held no fear for them, as they clearly remembered their past lives and knew that at the end of their biological body, a new life would bloom—a reflection of their spiritual journey and the aspirations they had cultivated.

An eternal joy of discovery and sharing permeated their existence. They respected the Whole, feeling themselves an integral part of all that exists, knowing they would always return.

One day, this paradise disappeared. The beings lost their memory of themselves and their powers. The separation from the Whole and from one another gave rise to fear and conflict. The world became dangerous, inhabited by unaware beings who hurt themselves, others, and nature.

Their power became a burden, abundance turned into insatiable desire, and so Atlantis sank into the depths.

Yet it was never truly lost. It lives in the hidden folds of our memories, in the depths of our spirit. Rediscovering Atlantis means rekindling the divine spark that lies within us, retracing the path back to the origin. To find it, you must look within yourself, descending into your personal depths, where the echoes of that ancient realm still resonate".

**Learner:** "It sounds like a lost dream... but how does this relate to me?"

**Master:** "Atlantis is not just a story; it is an archetype of your forgotten potential. Like the inhabitants of that realm, you possess incredible abilities and innate wisdom. But sometimes, just like them, you forget who you truly are. To rediscover Atlantis is to remember your power and your connection to the Whole."

Before diving into the world of Indigo souls, you might wonder how I came upon these realizations. Let me tell you a story.

Four years after that fleeting encounter on the bus, I had settled on the outskirts of Paris. Every day, I would seek a moment of peace by walking through a small park, its trees neatly arranged and its benches serene. I would pass under a railway underpass that opened, like a stage curtain, onto the serene view of a canal, the placid Seine, and the barges gliding slowly along it, almost as if suspended in a different time.

This place seemed to live by its own rules, governed by an arcane rhythm that only those who knew how to observe could perceive. Here, amid my steps and reflections, I loved to lose myself, as if the soul of Paris granted me a special privilege of introspection.

In these same spots once stood a noble residence that had hosted an illustrious Italian: the opera composer Gioachino Rossini[2].

Beyond a narrow pedestrian bridge, on the opposite bank, there was an abandoned garden with a gravel floor, where a curious mosaic of the sun could be found. It reminded me of The Sun card from the Major Arcana of the Tarot, which symbolizes, among other things, positive change. I learned this when I was introduced to the art of Tarot reading in an unnamed bar in Paris—a moment that, like the mosaic, felt both mysterious and illuminating.

---

[2] Gioachino Rossini, a brilliant composer with a free and original character, was a creator who transcended the limits of his time. He demonstrated remarkable independence of spirit and an extraordinary capacity for innovation. Through his music, he embodied profound sensitivity, boundless creativity, and a constant desire to challenge established norms.

Freshly certified as a personal coach and trainer, this milestone marked the beginning of a period of exploration and transformation. I had no idea of the challenges I would face, but that is another story. For now, I want to share with you my desire to help others.

The more I had opportunities to organize training events and connect with people, or to meet clients in one-on-one coaching sessions, the more I learned myself. Among the many individuals I encountered, some shared similar struggles and exhibited remarkably similar qualities.

These individuals were particularly sensitive, deeply committed to a journey of self-discovery, and eager to understand their life purpose. They seemed markedly more aware than those around them, displaying heightened consciousness and an unrelenting pursuit of truth and meaning.

Often gifted with profound empathy and strong intuition, these people demonstrated a genuine interest in personal and spiritual growth. They were constantly striving to deepen their understanding of the world and their place within it, driven by a heartfelt desire to make a positive contribution to their community.

Their ability to grasp the nuances of life and their deep desire to connect with others made them unique and invaluable.

The more I studied these traits, the more I began to encounter information about Indigos. Slowly, I could put a name to realities I had already come to understand in my daily life.

At first, I wasn't sure what I was doing. Doubts often crept in—I felt the imposter syndrome looming, questioning whether what I was doing truly had any meaning.

However, as I delved deeper into the reality of Indigos, an awareness began to grow within me. I realized I was embarking on something far greater than myself, something with planetary significance.

Perhaps you've felt this way, too. Perhaps there's been a time in your life when a new door opened, and suddenly coincidences began to appear—each one imbued with a sense of profound meaning. Someone mentions a topic you've been pondering, you hear a radio broadcast addressing your thoughts, or an overheard conversation seems to align perfectly with what's on your mind.

I will explore the concept of synchronicity in more detail later, but for now, I invite you to recall a time when such phenomena manifested in your life. Think about the emotions and feelings you experienced in those moments.

Synchronicities—those meaningful coincidences that seem to defy the laws of chance—often have a profound impact on our emotional state and our perception of reality. When you think back to such an experience, try to remember the precise details: what exactly happened, how you interpreted the event at the time, and how it influenced your perspective afterward.

The emotions tied to these experiences can vary, from surprise and curiosity to a deep sense of joy and connection. By reflecting on these moments, we can better understand the importance and meaning of synchronicities in our daily lives.

Imagine each new piece of information you receive, every discovery you make, as a light gradually illuminating your path. Move forward with confidence, feeling increasingly aligned with your true purpose. Feel this inner light growing within you, guiding you toward a deeper understanding of your role in this universe.

As you continue to explore, you'll notice that every detail, every trait you observe in others, becomes a piece of a larger puzzle. The more you learn, the more you realize that you are exactly where you need to be. Doubts fade, replaced by quiet certainty and renewed trust in yourself.

This is the reason I began my journey into the world of Indigos. I felt a deep connection with their traits and energy. I wrote this book to share the knowledge I've gathered over the years and to convey the results of my research.

As these words took shape and were reread countless times, a profound affection for Indigos gradually took root within me. The key to truly understanding this text lies in inner exploration, in gently examining the depths of our being, and in making a personal decision to embrace—or reject—that infinite force that resides within each of us.

This is an introspective journey, inviting each individual to dive into the heart of their own experiences and perceptions.

By embracing this inner quest, we can uncover hidden truths, awaken our latent potential, and establish a deeper connection with the Universe.

It is a journey to determine whether we are ready to weave the fabric of our dreams, no matter how impossible, magnificent, or daring they may seem. It is a journey that challenges societal judgment—that subtle yet oppressive weight borne by those who dare to aspire toward their most authentic dreams, pushing past conventions and beyond the limits of the ordinary.

In a world long shrouded in darkness, I am certain that each of us has, at some point, become aware of this shadow. But today marks the end of the tunnel. Many souls have awakened and now possess the ability to illuminate their own path. Having experienced the joy of living in balance between shadow and light, they can no longer settle for anything less than what is intrinsically true, powerful, and vibrant.

# 3 WHAT IS AN INDIGO ADULT?

*"It is very important to remember that what you seek is seeking you"*. – Rûmî

*"When you realize you lack nothing, the whole world belongs to you"*. – Lao Tzu

*"Spirituality requires, above all, a cultivation of the heart, immense strength, and unwavering courage. Cowards cannot fulfill a moral life"*. – Mohandas Karamchand (Gandhi)


I cannot explain why these memories linger. I belong to the category of so-called "black sheep." This awareness began to take root in me very early, even during my first years in kindergarten, where I often faced stern reprimands.

My parents had enrolled me in a religious school alongside many other children. I formed a bond with one of them—a quiet child who spoke very little. Perhaps because of this, the others isolated us. From a young age, I found myself gravitating toward people who were considered unusual, unique, or on the fringes of social norms.

The problem was, I struggled to conform to rules imposed authoritatively or those whose general utility I could not understand. This trait began causing issues very early on, as I mentioned, at that religious school where I was regularly punished.

The reason?

I simply refused to pray.

The idea of reciting "magic formulas" I couldn't understand, in unison with other children, was unbearable to me. As a child, the only way I could express my disagreement was through tears. At the beginning of every prayer session, I would burst into tears and stop only when it was over.

The nuns punished me by isolating me from the others. My "prison" was a corridor where I sat alone, surrounded by images of Pinocchio.

*"You're just like Pinocchio—you'll turn into a donkey,"* they told me.

Through my tears, I thought:

*"I feel so alone. No one loves me. There must be something wrong with me."*

Sometimes, I would wonder:

*"How long will this punishment last this time?"*

Eventually, you might not believe it, I started isolating myself voluntarily, both at school and at home. This feeling of not belonging, of not finding my place in the world, grew over time and stayed with me throughout my school years.

Have you ever felt this way?

As I grew older, this need to share what was within me—my thoughts, my intuitions—persisted. Yet, without like-minded souls who could understand me, I often retreated into solitude again.

My journey began in the shadows, where my thoughts whispered their stories, and the world seemed distant and indifferent. Each step carried the weight of isolation, a self-imposed exile from the symphony of life. At times, I felt like a modern hermit—minus the long beard and leather sandals.

Yet, within this cocoon of isolation, a subtle transformation took place. The echoes of my thoughts became faithful companions, and silence turned into a canvas for introspection. Through self-discovery, I began unraveling the chains that bound me to isolation. My soul, once wandering, found roots in self-awareness, and my spirit began to shine with a new light. Who would have thought silence could be so eloquent?

By embracing our fears and the traumas tied to our sensitivity, we can create a more aware personality and rewrite our personal story.

It's all about energy. As soon as we stop judging and simply allow ourselves to feel, we pave the way for transformation. I realized that what we resist persists. Resistance is a brake we impose on ourselves, preventing us from living authentically. Conversely, I began to feel capable of soaring, sensing in a subtle but unmistakable way—clear to the soul—that I was protected.

I've faced my personal "dark night of the soul" many times. Instead of perishing in the shadows, I discovered a better version of myself. By opening up to others, I found the profound beauty of vulnerability and the strength that lies in authenticity.

The path from solitude to openness is a metamorphosis that transcends the self. It is the recognition that growth arises from connection and that life's richness lies in the diversity of stories we share.

If you're holding this book, I think you can understand me perfectly. Perhaps you've lived, or are living, similar experiences.

Let me remind you of something I will repeat often in this book:

*"You are not alone."*

At 24, I attended a seminar on the "Law of Attraction." I found it incredibly inspiring and felt filled with positive energy. The conference hall was vast, surrounded by people diligently taking notes. I, on the other hand, preferred to listen with my eyes closed, trying to capture the deeper meaning of what was being shared.

The speaker, Esther, said:

*"Our thoughts are things, attracting what is similar to them."*

Reflecting on this, I wondered:

*"If that's true, what kind of life would we attract by surrendering to negative influences and events?"*

Then Esther added:

*"When we feel separate from others, isolated, or alone, we shut out the universe and prevent any help from entering our lives."*

Reading these words, you may feel something stir within you, as if a long-forgotten memory is resurfacing—ancestral, almost. Like a flickering light kindling in your heart, it may reveal, with surprising clarity, the realization that we have never been, nor will we ever be, truly alone.

The concept of "Indigo Souls" first emerged in the United States in the 1970s. Nancy Ann Tappe, a researcher with a rare perceptual ability, identified it. Tappe had inherited synesthesia from her grandmother—a neurobiological phenomenon where the senses intertwine, creating a symphony of perceptions.

Nancy could perceive the colorful auras surrounding people and "taste" shapes. When eating, colors and geometric forms appeared to her, mysteriously linked to flavors, suggesting a hidden order grasped only in the most intuitive moments.

Modern science explains Nancy's abilities as accessing a mode of brain function that is typically unavailable to most people. Researchers worldwide are studying synesthesia, which is no longer as obscure as it once was.

Indigos are here to foster significant change—in the environment, politics, and society—paving the way for humanity's evolution toward a higher consciousness.

For the first time in my life, I no longer felt alone. I realized I was surrounded by other "soul seekers" like me. Esther concluded the seminar with a profound thought that marked my journey of personal growth:

***"It's not about doing but being. Listen to your body and emotions. Let joy and expansion guide you, not fear."***

An Indigo soul embodies mystery, intuition, creativity, and honesty. These individuals inspire the evolution of consciousness, respect for sensitivity, and moral integrity. They carry an innate wisdom and a drive to honor every form of life on this planet.

I often call them "artisans of light," for they are here to bring light, love, and healing to Earth. Through their journey of personal and spiritual transformation, they discover their true identity and the mission entrusted to them.

The indigo color symbolizes intuition, perception, and enlightened consciousness—allowing them to "see" beyond the five senses.

Nancy Ann Tappe's observations revealed that children identified as "Indigos" were extraordinary—their awareness and understanding far exceeded those of other children their age.

Whatever your life mission may be, every Indigo has a fundamental role to play for the planet; otherwise, they wouldn't be here.

I ask for a little more patience. I know I've touched on many topics without delving deeply into any of them. In the pages ahead, I will discuss each of these subjects in more detail. For now, I wanted to share some ideas that might resonate with you, that you may feel to be true, recognize in yourself, or wish to learn more about.

To conclude this chapter, I want to share with you a beautiful prayer for Indigos:

"**To you, who have apologized for far too long for your compassion,**
    **to you who ask forgiveness for being emotional or too empathetic,**
    **to you who worry when someone stops talking to you or ignores your message,**

to you who suffer when you can't understand why a friend doesn't return your smile or someone averts their gaze;

to you who have pushed people away because you didn't want them to feel the pain you were trying to endure alone;

I am sorry.

I truly am.

I'm sorry that you must live in a time that doesn't understand the beautiful soul you possess.

I'm sorry that you must exist in a world where people like you are scarce, a world that feels completely upside down.

And yet, this world needs you more than you could ever imagine.

Yes, it needs you, because you instinctively give without asking for anything in return,

because you choose the harder path to put others' needs before your own.

You are a perfect example of raw authenticity, deeply in tune with your emotions, unafraid to be kind and vulnerable in a world filled with masked emotions.

You are a role model, proof for others that it's perfectly normal to be a living, imperfect soul.

This is for you, who are tired of apologizing for your vulnerability,

for you who go out of your way to tell someone you love them, for you who can't help but give more of yourself to others, even when all you have is yourself.

To you who have believed, and continue to believe, that people can grow and heal, that they just need love to bring out their best version.

Please, don't let the world tell you who you must be or who you cannot become.

Please, don't let pain or heartbreak force you to build walls of doubt and mistrust.

Please, keep giving, keep loving, keep believing that people can be better than they were yesterday, and never tire of being generous so others may find strength in your presence.

It's unavoidable: some people may not love you, they may criticize you, and your kindness might even be used against you.

I don't know the exact reasons of the Universe, but I know

that many people admire you, and some even wish they could be like you.

**Perhaps the Universe is harsh because it uses you as a source of inspiration**— so that other lost souls might continue to fight, to live, having an example to guide them as they rebuild their lives.

I admire you.

**I'm proud that you have survived, that you are alive, and that you continue to spread love, even when everything around you seems determined to corrupt or destroy you**»[3].

One final note: it is important to acknowledge that the concepts of Indigo adults and children are controversial and not grounded in solid scientific evidence. However, as I have already mentioned, I invite you to embrace what resonates with you—what you deeply feel to be true for yourself—and let go of the rest. There are many paths; find your own.

---

[3] This text is a beautiful prayer for Indigos. I did not write it; it circulates online and perfectly captures the spirit of this book. Perhaps it is a free expression of the collective unconscious or a poem whose author was lost amidst countless shares. If you are the author, or if you know who they are, I would love to thank you.

## 4. THE TRAITS THAT CONFIRM YOU ARE AN INDIGO ADULT

*"Take the blue pill, the story ends. You wake up in your bed and believe whatever you want to believe. Take the red pill, you stay in Wonderland, and I show you how deep the rabbit hole goes."* – Iconic quote by Morpheus in The Matrix

*"Our deepest fear is not that we are inadequate. Our deepest fear is that we are powerful beyond measure. It is our light, not our darkness, that most frightens us."* – Marianne Williamson

*"When we transcend humanity, then we shall be the Man."* – Sri Aurobindo

**Learner:** "I feel like I'm constantly reliving the same situations, as if I'm trapped in a cage."
**Master:** "Life is a journey filled with moments of joy and serenity, but also challenges and doubts. At times, it may seem like it places obstacles in our path, as though we are caught in a vortex, unable to see clearly. Yet, within you, there is a light, a strength that guides you, even when everything seems dark."
**Learner:** "All I feel is doubt, and I'm afraid that by choosing, I'll regret what I have to let go of."
**Master:** "These moments of uncertainty are a natural part of your growth and self-awareness. As a mystic named Gurdjieff taught, they often arise from inner conflict between the various parts of our being, shaped by the 'inner voices' and stories we tell ourselves. This

inner fragmentation creates 'confusion,' clouding our ability to see clearly.

Confusion is fueled by our mechanical nature—the tendency to react automatically to thoughts and emotions conditioned by past experiences and acquired beliefs. This reinforces our need for control and amplifies our fears, keeping us distant from the serenity and clarity that can only emerge when we cease identifying with these automatic reactions."

**Learner:** "So, there's no solution? What should I do?"

**Master:** "There is a path to dissipate this confusion and reconnect with your authentic essence. The first step is to recognize and disidentify from the internal narratives that obscure your perception. This means returning to the silent, unchanging center within you, where your essence resides beyond all stories and interpretations.

This essence is not a specific thought or emotion—it is the simple awareness of being, a subtle, harmonious vibration often hidden beneath the noise of identifications and the tales we tell ourselves.

To connect with this essence, observe and feel the reactions that arise in response to your narratives, letting them flow as pure energy. It doesn't matter if these emotions are pleasant or painful: welcome them and transform them into vital energy. By directing your conscious attention to this fundamental state of being, you begin to separate yourself from the identifications and distortions that generate confusion.

This practice allows you to embrace your emotions and reactions without judgment, seeing them as temporary manifestations of energy. Over time, you will cultivate a stable presence and a deeper connection with your authentic essence, freeing yourself from the weight of mental and emotional constructs that distance you from clarity and serenity."

**Learner:** "And how can I overcome the confusion? If I understand correctly, I'll never truly be myself or be free!"

**Master:** "As you develop this ability to detach, the confusion will begin to subside. Over time, you will be able to follow what truly makes you happy deep down, beyond external beliefs and conventions. This will allow you to live fully in harmony with your true nature."

As I mentioned earlier, I became deeply interested in the topic of Indigo adults, devouring all the available literature and interviewing people who had been on this journey long before I started my research. However, I still wanted to learn more:

*"Who are these Indigos?"*

*"How can they be helped to understand that there's nothing wrong with them?"*

*"How can they recognize themselves for who they truly are?"*

Years had passed. I was now living in the French countryside, and as I walked through a field with my dog, these same questions kept echoing in my mind.

The air felt crisp and alive, carrying the invigorating scent of meadows that seemed to awaken forgotten memories. The gentle rustling of leaves whispered timeless secrets, while the soft murmur of a hidden stream, just beyond the trees, seemed to call out, inviting a sense of calm and connection to something greater.

*"What does it mean to recognize oneself?"*

This question had been posed to me during a seminar on the subject. For me, the answer is both simple and essential: we can only truly desire something, live a life that authentically represents us, and love sincerely if we manage to remember who we really are.

I had a profound interest in the Hermetic laws and their connection to certain historical monuments, which seemed to encode these principles as silent and eternal witnesses to their presence.

The Hermetic principles, rooted in the ancient wisdom attributed to Hermes Trismegistus, encompass seven universal laws governing the cosmos and human existence. These principles—including the Laws of Mentalism, Correspondence, Vibration, Polarity, Rhythm, Cause and Effect, and Gender—offer profound insights into the nature of reality and the interconnectedness of all things.

The Cathedral of Chartres, a masterpiece of Gothic architecture in France, fascinatingly embodies these Hermetic concepts. Its design and symbolic elements—from the intricate labyrinth on its floor to the celestial alignment of its structure—reflect a deep understanding of the principles of correspondence and vibration. The cathedral's renowned stained glass windows and sculptures are not just artistic marvels but also testify to the medieval synthesis of spirituality and science, echoing the Hermetic belief in harmony between the divine and the earthly.

I often visited the Cathedral of Chartres, captivated by the presence of deep wells dug by the Celts, now integrated into the cathedral's foundations, which seemed like a magnificent antenna capable of channeling energy. Initially, these visits were personal, but as I developed my knowledge and better understood the fusion of energetic symbols and architecture, friends began accompanying me. Soon, these outings turned into full-fledged guided tours, and I found myself acting as an expert, sharing my discoveries and passion with others.

The Carnutes, a Gallic tribe, used this site for religious ceremonies, believing it to be a point of spiritual energy emanation from the underground. Around these wells, they erected menhirs and dolmens to channel divine energy during their sacred practices. As I delved deeper into the mysteries of Chartres Cathedral, I realized that this place also embodies Gnostic principles. Its very architecture—with its labyrinths, stained glass windows, and geometric patterns—seems to invite the seeker to uncover hidden knowledge, or gnosis, transcending the material world.

In Gnostic traditions, enlightenment occurs through the discovery of inner light, and similarly, Chartres uses natural light, filtered through its magnificent stained glass windows, to symbolize the divine presence guiding every soul toward deeper understanding. Thus, Chartres is not merely a religious monument; it is a space of personal transformation, reflecting humanity's eternal quest for spiritual awakening. Walking through its sacred aisles, one cannot help but sense a crossroads between the visible and the invisible, between ancient wisdom and the inner journey that connects all souls in search of truth. This sacred site invites visitors to contemplate the mysteries of the universe, encouraging an inner pilgrimage akin to the spiritual journey described in Hermetic teachings.

One of these Hermetic principles states:

*"That which is below is like that which is above, and that which is above is like that which is below."*

At this point in your reading, you might find yourself with questions or doubts, such as:

*"Why am I different from others?"*
*"Am I an Indigo?"*
*"What does it mean?"*
*"Are there others like me?"*

Some people discover they are Indigo from a young age, while others need more time to understand their nature. In this chapter, I have summarized the key characteristics of Indigo adults, which will help you determine with reasonable certainty whether you might be one. As I describe these characteristics, I encourage you to pay attention to what resonates within you, without fixating too much on each individual trait. Instead, recognize what aligns with what you feel to be true, as it reflects what you already know deep inside. Just as the spiritual energies of ancient Druids still linger beneath Chartres Cathedral, the profound truths of Indigos can be found by listening to our intuition and recognizing what touches us deeply.

In the following pages, I will share what I have learned about Indigos and provide tools to help you reflect on what you already know about yourself.

One last note: it is quite common for an Indigo to resist identifying with the label. The essential question lies in their profound essence, which does not require definitions. Indigos often feel an inner calling to transcend societal classifications and categories. Their true nature is that of spiritual explorers, seeking a broader understanding of their existence and place in the universe. Accepting or rejecting the term "Indigo" does not change their essence; what matters is the recognition and exploration of their true identity and spiritual mission.

To begin this journey, I invite you to take a simple test. If you recognize yourself in the following fourteen signs, it is highly likely that you are an Indigo.

## 1. If You Were Born in 1978 or Later

This is the period when Nancy Ann Tappe began studying the Indigo phenomenon. It's important to note that Indigos existed even before this time, but the late 1970s marked the beginning of a more visible and widespread manifestation of this phenomenon. Thus, even if you were born before 1978, the "Indigo wave" studied by Nancy Ann Tappe gained momentum during this period. While they have always been present throughout history, these years saw an unusual intensification and concentration of these exceptional souls, sparking greater interest in understanding their nature and their role in humanity's evolving consciousness.

Remember that every individual is unique: being born before 1978 does not exclude the possibility of sharing Indigo characteristics. The studies from that era simply provide a reference point for understanding the increased influx of these souls from that time onward.

## 2. You Value Free Thinking

You prefer to form your own opinions and act according to what you feel is right, even if it requires making sacrifices. You have an innate inclination to question established norms and constantly explore beyond imposed limits, challenging dogmas accepted by the majority. Instead of passively accepting the prevailing "truth" often regarded as sacred and unchangeable, you actively seek alternative perspectives, embracing a free and independent mindset.

This need for free thinking, if you are not aligned with who you are and what you truly love, may sometimes leave you feeling lost, unable to find your place in the world.

## 3. You Embody a Nonconformist Spirit

You naturally embody a nonconformist spirit, driven by an inner force that resists imposed rules and aspires to define your own path in the world. From an early age, your relationship with authority—starting with your parents—has often been marked by subtle but decisive rebellion, especially during the period when you lived under their roof. It's within this tension with authority that you discovered your ability to question rules, push boundaries, and consider alternative perspectives.

However, this nonconformism, if untempered, may lead you to distrust others, struggle to find common ground with them, and face challenges in building a sense of belonging within a community. This could undermine your potential for happiness and limit your ability to unleash your unique talents.

## 4. You've Always Had an Uncommon Wisdom

From the very beginning of your life, you've carried an extraordinary wisdom that transcends conventional understanding. You focus on what truly matters, paying attention to the essence of things that resonate deeply with your being. Your gaze penetrates beyond the superficial, capturing the true substance of experiences and relationships. In contemplating what holds authentic value, you find strength and inspiration.

It's important to recognize that if you are not aligned with your true essence, this trait can lead to intense inner conflicts, particularly when faced with significant life decisions.

## 5. Rigid Discipline and Predefined Rules Are Not for You

Imposed rules and rigid discipline are not your strong suit. Rather than fostering growth, these impositions cause you distress or provoke an irresistible urge to fight for your freedom. You are an indomitable spirit, determined to forge your own path and categorically refusing to conform to limiting and meaningless norms. For you, every rule represents a barrier to your innate freedom, an invitation to creative rebellion.

As a result, your life becomes a continuous quest for freedom, a resolute will to emancipate yourself from conventions.

If you are not connected to your true nature, this characteristic may lead you to feel isolated and struggle to find balance with those around you. Building harmonious relationships can be challenging without a stable foundation of love, respect, unity, and acceptance of differences.

## 6. You Vibrate at a Higher Energy Level than Those Around You

Your energy transcends conventional boundaries, vibrating at levels much higher than the norm. This elevated vibrational state places you in spheres of higher energy, endowing you with a charisma that naturally inspires those fortunate enough to encounter you. People are often instinctively drawn to you.

However, this exceptional energy can also attract negative personalities, such as "energy vampires," who consciously or unconsciously seek to feed on your vitality and light. If you are unaware of this, it can lead to significant stress and frustration in both your personal and professional life. To protect yourself, you may have learned to become "invisible," revealing your true energy only when necessary or when in the company of those who genuinely appreciate and accept you for who you are at your core. This allows you to avoid the constant need for self-protection.

## 7. You Are "Emotionally Reactive"

You act as a receiver of energies, capable of absorbing the subtle nuances of the universe around you. This sensitivity connects you deeply to the essence of life itself, allowing you to perceive even the slightest shifts in energy around you. However, this receptivity also exposes you to the emotional turbulence of others, causing you to absorb negative energies that many might not even notice. In a way, you are an "emotional sponge," absorbing both positive and negative vibrations with surprising intensity.

Despite the challenges this sensitivity brings, it is precisely this ability that makes you unique. As an Indigo, your strength lies in your capacity to transform these energies into creative expressions, converting difficulties into opportunities for personal growth. You are an energy catalyst, capable of turning negative vibrations into positive forces that can inspire and guide those around you.

However, if you are not yet aware of this condition, you might absorb others' negative energies and suffer because of it. This could lead to anxiety, depression, or even outbursts of anger, especially when you are energetically out of balance. In the upcoming chapters, I will provide more tools to help you understand and better manage this sensitivity.

## 8. You Have a High Potential

You have the ability to shift seamlessly between the right hemisphere of your brain, associated with creativity, and the left hemisphere, associated with rationality. Your exceptional potential lies in this extraordinary capacity to alternate between the two, blending prolific creativity with precise rationality. As an Indigo adult, you are a multidimensional being capable of merging artistic intuition with advanced analytical thought.

However, it's important to recognize that traditional education systems may not have always appreciated or nurtured your abilities and inclinations. School and university might not have been designed to value them. Your academic years could have been marked by boredom, a sense of disconnection from conventional teaching methods, and occasional challenges caused by anxiety or difficulties adapting. Diagnoses like Attention Deficit Disorder (ADD) may have been attributed to your Indigo nature, where your rapid thinking and ability to process information faster than average were mistaken for mere impulsivity. In reality, this demonstrates your intellectual vibrancy, not a deficit.

## 9. Your Actions Stem from Your Choices, Reasoning, and, Most Importantly, Intuitions

You unconsciously comprehend what others often fail to grasp, thanks to a harmonious fusion of resolute choices, reasoned deliberations, and, above all, profound intuitions. Your understanding goes beyond the limits of ordinary consciousness, delving into the mysterious corners of the unconscious.

You perceive the subtle energies that animate the world and understand the profound implications of every choice. It is within these mystical spaces of the unconscious that you find answers to questions that often perplex more conventional minds. You are guided by a sixth sense, an inner compass that always points to the truth, even when this truth is hidden from others—or even from yourself, especially when you are not yet ready to accept something about yourself or those close to you.

## 10. You Are Either Vegetarian, Vegan, Or Particularly Conscious About Your Diet.

You seek to nourish yourself with healthy, energy-rich foods, such as organic produce, because you understand that food is more than mere sustenance—it is a source of information and energy for your body. Your relationship with food transcends the act of eating; it represents a conscious manifestation of your commitment to health, energy, and respect for life.

You avoid unhealthy food and excesses, aware of the impact they can have on your energy and overall well-being. Your preference for healthy and nutritious foods reflects a deep understanding of the connection between what you consume and your physical, mental, and spiritual health.

## 11. You Oscillate Between Feelings Of Low Self-Esteem And An Overconfident Attitude That Can Occasionally Come Across As Arrogant

You've always navigated between grand aspirations and fluctuating self-esteem. You harbor significant ambitions and a desire to change the world and challenge the status quo, yet you often doubt your abilities. Your inner journey is a complex dance between shadow and light, where your self-perception oscillates between modesty and confidence.

This duality, however, creates a delicate balance. Your burning desire to challenge the status quo is occasionally interrupted by moments of hesitation—a reluctance to fully believe in your ability to achieve your ambitions.

It's important to view this duality not as a conflict but as a fascinating dynamic of your inner being. These oscillations between modesty and audacity are a fundamental part of your journey. By embracing this duality, you can find a harmonious balance where your self-esteem grows through the acknowledgment of your ambitions, and vice versa.

## 12. You May Suffer from Insomnia, Sleep Disorders, or Nightmares

It's possible that you wake up in the middle of the night, screaming. This becomes even more likely if you haven't yet had the opportunity to fully be yourself or express your potential due to certain limiting factors in your current life—your job, your environment, or the place where you live. That nighttime scream breaking the silence resonates as a call from your soul, a powerful reminder of the need to free yourself.

These limiting factors, stemming from work, your surroundings, or where you live, act as barriers that hold back the natural flow of your Indigo energy. This scream becomes one of resistance, an abrupt awakening against the chains that block your potential—a signal from those "night demons" that visit you in your sleep when your defenses are weakest, feeding on your energy.

## 13. You May Suffer from Depression or Have Had Suicidal Thoughts

If this is the case, know that you are not alone, and there are better ways to bring meaning to your life! Darkness may sometimes envelop your being, and the whispers of depression can attempt to smother the light of your Indigo soul. Suicidal thoughts, like a dark vortex, may seek to disturb your mind's peace.

In these challenging moments, it's essential to understand that you are not alone. Invisible bonds connect you to other Indigo souls who may have felt this same oppressive weight. You are stronger than you believe, and darkness cannot extinguish the light that resides within you.

Remember that your life has immense value and that there are infinite possibilities for transformation and growth. You are a unique being, carrying a special light capable of illuminating even the darkest corners of your existence. Recognizing your suffering and despair is the first step toward healing.

Do not fear sharing your burden with those around you. Seek professional support and explore the paths of therapy and personal development. Every small step forward is a victory over the darkness. Know that your existence profoundly impacts the world around you and that your light, once freed, can illuminate the way for others traversing similar shadows.

## 14. Some of the Rules You're Obligated to Follow Seem Ridiculous

You want to live life your way, but this isn't always accepted by others At the core of your Indigo being, you feel a repulsion for certain rules that seem to confine you to narrow limits. Society's impositions often appear meaningless, and the idea of adhering to norms that don't reflect your true essence stirs an inner rebellion.

You deeply feel the need to live according to your principles, to carve out your own path, to dance to the unique rhythm of your melody. However, this aspiration for an authentic existence, free from chains, is often misunderstood or poorly received by those around you. Society has its rules and norms, and your desire to challenge them can sometimes create friction with those who are more inclined to accept the status quo.

Beyond the fields, accompanied by my faithful Buddy, a cold, strong wind howled despite the sun shining brightly in the sky. Drawn to the welcoming warmth of my fireplace, I decided to head back home.

Seated before the fire, I watch the flames dance, cradled by a tranquility spreading from my heart to my head, enveloping every part of my body.

The hypnotic effect of the flames begins to warm not only my body but also my soul. It feels as though that warmth has the power to melt away every tension that has accumulated within me. A profound sense of peace invades my being, as though the cold wind had carried not only its sharp chill but also a serene harmony.

The flickering light of the flames becomes a form of meditation, a personal ritual of relaxation. The contrast between the biting cold outside and the comforting warmth of the fire inside creates a perfect balance—a magical atmosphere that allows my mind to wander freely.

The house, my dog sleeping soundly by my side, and the glittering fire form a living tableau—a scene in which I find myself completely immersed. In this moment of stillness, I realize that the connection with nature and the magic of fire rejuvenate me, preparing me for the adventures the future holds. There's no need to force anything; everything seems to unfold naturally.

I've come to understand that if I have a role to play in this story of the Indigos, it will all reveal itself in due time, taking shape and substance in my life.

As the fire crackles softly, its warmth lulling me into a serene state, I drift to sleep. A quiet awareness lingers—a knowing that new adventures await me in my quest to understand and share the knowledge of these exceptional souls: the Indigo adults.

# 5 THE SECOND TEST: ARE YOU AN INDIGO ADULT?

At this point, you might already have some awareness regarding your identity as an Indigo. However, the following test is designed to deepen this understanding, exploring various aspects of your personality, experiences, and perception of the world—elements that may align with the characteristics of Indigo adults.

Answer honestly and spontaneously to the questions. You are about to embark on a journey of self-exploration, and I invite you to approach it with openness and curiosity. Happy introspection!

1. Do you feel a profound sense of disconnection from your existence and daily surroundings?
   YES / NO

2. Do you often feel detached, as if you're on the fringes of the reality around you?
   YES / NO

3. Do you sometimes feel that your true place is elsewhere, in a space that resonates more authentically with your inner being?
   YES / NO

4. Does your life often feel imbued with a uniqueness that defies immediate understanding, sparking a constant search for meaning and belonging?
YES / NO

5. Do you sometimes feel out of sync with or reluctant to conform to society's expectations regarding relationships, money, and work?
YES / NO

6. Do you experience a certain dissonance between traditional societal obligations and your true nature, prompting ongoing reflection on how you want to engage with the world?
YES / NO

7. Do you experience anxiety during moments of separation?
YES / NO

8. Do moments of separation, whether from loved ones, familiar places, or significant experiences, cause you a sense of distress?
YES / NO

9. Do you find yourself worried at times about losing important connections or distancing yourself from what you hold dear?
YES / NO

10. Do separations, whether temporary or permanent, evoke a particular emotional response in you, highlighting the depth of your emotional bonds and sensitivity?
YES / NO

11. Do you sometimes feel as if you don't quite belong on this Earth?
YES / NO

12. Do you feel a sense of feeling out of place, as if your roots don't fully anchor you in the reality you live in?
YES / NO

13. Do you find yourself questioning your role and the meaning of this vast world, seeking a deeper purpose for your existence?
YES / NO

14. Do you often feel that this sense of not being fully aligned with your surroundings leads you to reflect deeply on your origins and ultimate destination?
YES / NO

15. Does the concept of justice hold an important place in your life, evoking a strong attachment to ethics and equality?
YES / NO

16. Do you harbor a profound sense of justice, as if your soul is naturally inclined to respond to injustices?
YES / NO

17. Does your pursuit of justice frequently influence your decisions and actions, pushing you to oppose the injustices you see around you?
YES / NO

18. Do you have an extraordinary imagination?
YES / NO

19. Are you highly sensitive?
YES / NO

20. Are you naturally perseverant, to the point of becoming almost "obsessed" with your ideas?
YES / NO

21. Do you often have big plans, a grand vision of things?
YES / NO

22. Do you easily find solutions to problems through the power of your intuition?
YES / NO

23. Are you naturally curious?
    YES / NO

24. Are you very quick, or even hyperactive?
    YES / NO

25. Are you gifted with mental agility and/or extraordinary intuition?
    YES / NO

26. Have you always felt like you have a mission and that your presence here is not by chance?
    YES / NO

27. Do you find it difficult or almost impossible to lie, even when you feel forced to?
    YES / NO

28. Are you creative?
    YES / NO

29. Does it come naturally to you to care for others?
    YES / NO

30. Do you sometimes feel a sense of superiority over the people around you?
    YES / NO

31. Do you feel a sense of rebellion when situations or conditions seem unfair to you?
    YES / NO

32. Do you express this sense of rebellion?
    YES / NO

33. Do you find it hard to accept constraints, rules, and external discipline?
    YES / NO

34. Do you pay close attention to your diet?

YES / NO

35. Do you feel like you have extrasensory abilities?
    YES / NO

36. Do you feel disconnected from your life or surroundings?
    YES / NO

37. Do you feel uncomfortable with the constraints imposed by certain social, economic, or professional conventions?
    YES / NO

38. Do you always have big plans, a grand vision of things?
    YES / NO

If you answered "yes" to 24 or more of these questions, it is very likely that you are an Indigo adult.

# 6 THIRD TEST TO BETTER UNDERSTAND YOUR INDIGO IDENTITY

If you're still unsure, I'd like to offer you a third test to gain a clearer understanding.

Below, you'll find ten challenges that Indigo adults commonly experience. If you relate to these struggles, there's a strong likelihood that you may be an Indigo adult:

### 1. You feel ahead of your time

You often feel as though you belong to a different era, with ideas that are too advanced or innovative for the society around you. This sensation creates a sense of distance from conventional thinking, as if your way of being clashes with the reality you live in. You carry within you a vision that seems too futuristic to be fully understood or accepted, leaving you feeling at times like a pioneer, and at others, misunderstood.

### 2. You struggle to find your place

This sense of misalignment drives you to constantly search for a space—real or symbolic—where you can feel truly in tune with yourself and others. Your search is relentless, and at times it leaves you with a sense of isolation, as though the world around you cannot fully embrace your essence.

### 3. People have tried to figure out what's "wrong" with you

From a young age, those around you have sought to interpret your differences, sometimes perceiving you as a difficult or problematic child. Your sensitivity, deep thoughts, and unconventional reactions to the world often unsettled them, leading them to attempt to fit you into molds that didn't resonate with your true self.

### 4. Your choices have worried others

Your life decisions, worldview, or way of approaching situations have often caused concern among those around you. Your desire to follow unconventional paths or distance yourself from established expectations has frequently fueled anxieties about your future and your approach to life.

### 5. You feel like others don't understand you, and you sometimes feel alone

You often feel profoundly alone, as though no one around you can truly grasp who you are or understand what you feel. This emotional distance can weigh heavily on your spirit, pushing you to seek out people who can share authentic thoughts and experiences with you.

### 6. You've realized much of what you were taught was an illusion

Over time, you've started to notice the cracks in the beliefs, principles, and teachings passed on to you. They often seem built on illusions or distorted interpretations of reality. This realization has led you to question everything, embarking on a journey of discovery to find a truth that genuinely reflects your inner feelings and perceptions.

### 7. You absorb other people's emotions

You are deeply empathetic, feeling the emotions of others intensely. This sensitivity can make you vulnerable to their pain or moods. It's often difficult to protect yourself from these emotional influences because you naturally absorb the energies around you, which can leave you emotionally drained. However, this sensitivity also allows you to understand and support others in exceptional ways.

### 8. You know everything is connected

You have an innate sense that everything in the universe is interconnected, that even the smallest action has consequences, and that we are all part of a greater whole. This awareness gives you a special sensitivity to the world and a profound sense of belonging to something larger, where every gesture impacts the collective.

### 9. The thought of monotonous work feels like slow death

The idea of a routine job with rigid hours and repetitive tasks feels like a slow demise to you. It stifles your creativity and your need for freedom, limiting your potential and preventing you from thriving in pursuits that you truly love.

### 10. Sometimes, you feel completely exhausted

There are times when you feel utterly overwhelmed, as though your emotions, thoughts, and the constant pressure of the outside world become an unbearable weight. This feeling of being overloaded can occur frequently, pulling you into an inner whirlwind that feels difficult to manage. The expectations of others and the demands of daily life can quickly drain your energy, leaving you with a deep need to retreat to your private space and take a step back to recharge.

It's during these moments that you recognize the importance of reconnecting with your essence, finding the inner balance that allows you to realign with your true self. Whether it's through nature, meditation, or simply taking time for yourself, this need to center yourself becomes vital for preserving your well-being and peace of mind in a world that sometimes feels overwhelming.

Recognizing these challenges in your life can help you better understand your Indigo nature and how it shapes your way of experiencing the world. Allow this introspection to guide you toward uncovering deeper aspects of yourself.

Before concluding, I'd like to share one final characteristic, which I believe is the most enigmatic of all those I've described. For Indigo adults, the starry sky exerts a profound and mysterious fascination, evoking both awe and a sense of longing.

Contemplating the vastness of the universe and the immeasurable distances of the cosmos, they often feel an indescribable connection, as if that expanse calls to a place intimately familiar to them. This fascination transcends mere curiosity, awakening a yearning to reconnect with something greater than the earthly world. To them, the stars are not just luminous points in the sky; they are witnesses to a deeper spiritual origin, echoes of a cosmic home they seem to recognize. The immensity of space resonates with their quest for meaning and their sense of belonging to a larger mystery—a mystery that compels them to explore and reconnect with the cosmic forces guiding their journey in this life.

## 7 VOICES THAT REMIND YOU ARE NOT ALONE

*"It's never too late to be what you might have been."* – George Eliot

*"The greatest thing in the world is to know how to belong to oneself."* – Michel de Montaigne

*"Follow your bliss, and the universe will open doors for you where there were only walls."* – Joseph Campbell

**Master:** "If you don't walk toward yourself, you distance yourself from the one who can truly make you happy."
**Learner:** "What do you mean?" he asked, a puzzled look on his face.
**Master:** "Think about your true desires," he replied. "If you ignore them, it's like giving up on the chance to fully live, as if you're smothering the spark that makes you unique." The **Learner** fell silent for a moment, then whispered, "But how can I know what my true desires are?"
**Master:** "You must listen to your heart," he said with a gentle smile. "It's not easy to silence the expectations of others, I know. But only by doing so can you make room for the desires we often hide even from ourselves."
**Learner:** "And what happens when I recognize them?"
**Master:** "Then you will find the path to your fulfillment. You'll begin to embrace your true nature, and each step will bring you closer to a more authentic and satisfying life."

Years earlier, before becoming a coach and author, as I mentioned, I lived in Paris and had just started working for a large company. It didn't take long for me to realize that I couldn't keep living under the weight of expectations placed upon me: spending most of my life inside an office, doing a job I had studied and worked hard for, simply because that's what was expected of me.

Sitting in my office chair, my gaze was drawn to something outside the window. Right before me stood a blossoming cherry tree, its delicate branches bursting with life and color. Each petal seemed to express the simple, pure joy of being, like a silent invitation to reconnect with what truly matters.

While gazing at that scene, a clear thought crossed my mind, striking me with undeniable clarity: time would pass, and life would slip away without me—or rather, without the true me—because in that place, I could only exist as a very limited version of myself.

Deep within, an indescribable yearning consumed my soul, pushing me to break free from the chains of conformity and rediscover the true essence of my existence.

***"You look tired—another sleepless night?"*** a colleague asked.

***"Yes, again,"*** I replied with a sigh. ***"I've been having trouble sleeping lately."***

***"Well, if you don't sleep, you can't perform well. And we need results here,"*** she said, not even glancing in my direction.

I couldn't care less about "performance." I needed to figure out how to escape this situation and find myself again. I had to do it quickly because every day in that environment drained my energy further. Every day pulled me further away from myself.

I found myself trapped in a toxic office setting, engulfed in an oppressive, unhealthy atmosphere. Outside my window, the cherry tree stood tall and free, celebrating life with its vibrant blossoms, a silent hymn to joy and beauty. Meanwhile, I was forfeiting my own life. While the tree lived without fear, I remained a prisoner in a gray world, suffocated by routine and the weight of a toxic environment.

I could feel my life force being drained, all for the sake of earning enough to pay rent. I wasn't living the dream I had hoped for—a life where I could express my creativity and pursue my deepest aspirations.

Each passing day, this reality weighed on me more heavily, as though I were sinking into a dark abyss where the light of my being dimmed, stifled by the relentless demands of that cold, distant environment.

***"What am I doing here, wasting away in this misery?"***

Parallel to my anguish, the pain and solitude I felt drove me to seek inner peace, immersing myself in personal development and spirituality. It was during this period that I began writing a blog, publicly exploring the phenomenon of Indigo people.

In the excitement of my discoveries, I published my first article on "Indigo adults" for free on my blog. The piece quickly resonated with readers, revealing a community thirsty for truth. The responses I received felt like a refreshing rain, nourishing my soul and bringing profound gratitude. Every word I wrote on the blog brought me closer to my true essence, far from the emptiness of the corporate world.

The comments and testimonials from readers illuminated my path. They were like stars in the night, signs that I was not alone.

This book is dedicated to the truths and stories I've gathered. While I couldn't publish every account, each one has helped me grow. Names and personal details have been changed to preserve anonymity, but the stories remain powerful and illuminating. I sincerely thank all those who shared their experiences.

I invite you to immerse yourself in these testimonials and let their stories carry you. They show that you are not alone and that Indigo adults are among us. Together, we can create a brighter and transformative future.

I've summarized each testimony in a single sentence. You can stop at the excerpt or read the full comment, but it's important not to skip this part of the book. The key is understanding that there are many other Indigo adults out there right now, and they are all remarkably similar.

By sharing my journey and receiving the support of so many Indigo individuals, I found a new source of strength and inspiration. I hope these stories resonate with you and help you feel part of a community.

### Grace: "Understanding that I am an Indigo gives me immense relief and the courage to face depression and the negative energies of society."

"I've just realized that I'm an Indigo adult, born in 1975. It's such a relief to know that I'm not the only one feeling so disconnected from this society! I recognize myself in every single point you've addressed—it's incredible! I feel as if I've been guided here to better understand who I truly am; I have no doubt about it.

In fact, I've been immersed in a form of depression for several months, utterly exhausted by the negative energies, intolerance, and the blatant disregard this society shows for beauty, goodness, justice, and truth. Your article gives me courage and makes me believe in my ability to create the life I need for myself and others. It seems like a new beginning is emerging for me.

I just want to say a huge THANK YOU for being here and for being who you are. Nothing happens by chance. I hope to share my new life with you soon."

**Anna: "Discovering my Indigo nature helped me understand why I felt different, often misunderstood, and always driven to seek justice and well-being for animals while fighting against corruption and injustice."**

"Born in 1946, it was shortly after turning 35 that I realized I wasn't like 'everyone else'! People often called me a visionary, told me I was 'special but unable to adapt,' or a 'rebel' because I couldn't tolerate injustices of any kind. Even my mother occasionally called me 'odd'!

Since childhood, I've always felt a deep love for animals. Instinctively, I disliked eating meat. When I became fully aware of the immense suffering inflicted on animals, I quickly reduced my meat consumption and eventually stopped eating it entirely many years ago. Now, with all the terrible things being exposed—laboratories, slaughterhouses, abandonment, etc.—I know I'll never be truly happy because I'll pass away before these atrocities end!

I've helped many animals and people in need, feeling it was my duty. Every pet I've had was either adopted or found, and I've taken in so many over the years, back when there were fewer shelters and organizations than today. Currently, I still have three dogs—two adopted and one rescued from the street—and a cat I found in my garden as a kitten (she's now over three years old).

In short, I fully recognize myself in what you describe. I hate being forced to do things or obey authority (often unjust). Corruption enrages me. I can sense people even from a distance or through their writings, and I have premonitory dreams or flashes of insight. I often need time alone—it's the only way I can recharge (whether people like it or not!). I need to be surrounded by nature, and living in a city for years was a terrible nightmare for me…

I know my mission, even if it's very humble, and I will see it through! My calling is animals, with whom I feel an enormous bond, so much so that sometimes I think I'm a little animal-like myself!

One last thing: I feel uncomfortable in this world… For all the reasons you know. I struggle with certain people, especially those consumed by materialism."

## Camille: "Hypersensitivity and empathy, battling misunderstanding and depression, guided by love and the desire to help others."

"Hello, my name is Camille. This year I will turn 33, so I was born in 1991. Since adolescence, I've struggled with many things. At 15, I visited a chapel in Sainte-Anne d'Auray. I was overwhelmed by emotions—sadness and pain filled my entire body. I walked out in tears. The only person who believed me at the time was my father.

Since that experience, I've often felt isolated and misunderstood, living with hypersensitivity and empathy that cause me constant pain. I've faced depression many times, and even today, I feel misunderstood. I don't watch the news anymore because I cry in front of the screen—the world disgusts me, as do the judgments of people who fail to understand that love is essential and everything else is just material. I hate injustice and lies, and I can recognize good and evil in people. When I talk about these things with others, they think I'm crazy, but I feel simply more human. Even now, as I write, I'm in tears. I don't claim to be an Indigo—I don't reflect all the signs, and I'm cautious about certain beliefs—but reading this, I've finally felt understood.

I feel my purpose is to help others, and when I can't, I fight and never give up, even if it leaves me feeling exhausted. I live with a man who is struggling, and I suffer because of it, though he doesn't understand. My words often help others, and people come to me when they are feeling hurt or emotionally wounded. Despite my own pain, helping others makes me feel better.

I don't know if I'm an Indigo adult, but I consider myself more human than most people I know. Love guides my life, and I live for that and the good of others, even at the cost of forgetting myself.

Thank you for your work on Indigos—it has already helped me feel better and continue on my path with greater serenity and the same goal: to love and help make this world a better place."

**Jacob: "Discovering that I match 95% of the Indigo characteristics has shaken me, especially since I am not a 'spiritual' person at all."**

"Hello, I feel genuinely uncomfortable because, to be honest, I have no interest in the spiritual or related worlds and stumbled upon the concept of Indigos purely by chance. I'm not sure how to interpret this! I was born in 1967, and surprisingly, I align with 95% of the characteristics described. Without knowing anything about this, I believe I've suppressed it for decades, and it's incredibly strange and difficult to live with this realization! I won't go into detail—you'll understand—but yes, I'm tormented by visions of an impossible future and other things that serve me no purpose yet have been haunting me for about thirty years. It's all just too strange and unmanageable!"

**Jade: "I resonate deeply with managing excessive empathy and the importance of self-work."**

"Born in 1974, these aspects reflect my life. As for sleep, I generally rest well, except during REM sleep, where I receive a kind of 'communication' that I prefer not to engage with. I impose a degree of 'control' in other areas to mitigate the consequences of sometimes overwhelming empathy. Self-work and acceptance are essential. Thank you for your article."

**Jennifer: "I've always felt like I landed on the wrong planet, self-taught from a young age, and have struggled with depression and anxiety."**

"This resonates with me completely, even though I was born in 1977. From birth, I've had the distinct impression of being dropped onto the wrong planet. Self-taught in many areas, it's as if I already knew things I'd never seen before. I taught myself to read, garden, and cook by the age of six. I even excelled at learning foreign languages effortlessly. Often rejected and mistreated for this uniqueness, I gradually lost confidence in myself, eventually falling, according to some, into depression and anxiety. I spent time in a psychiatric clinic to reorient myself and understand my inner workings and the roots of my lifelong struggles. Additionally, I've experienced spiritual perceptions that add to the picture of my peculiarities, which I've only shared with a few open-minded individuals so far."

## Louise: "I'm learning to balance life's polarities, to appreciate the lessons in every challenge, and to share a universal love."

"From the signs I've observed, I believe I belong to the Indigo generation, as I was born in 1979. I've identified with many aspects and have started to understand that, like yin and yang, everything is tied to a polarity that allows us to find balance. Just as the sun without rain, joy without sadness, or light without shadow would lack meaning or emotional resonance… This state of awareness brings a calming realization, enabling me to accept and appreciate, with humility, all that contributes to life's learning—through what we see, sense, and perceive—to give, share, and balance that imperceptible love we hope will become universal. It's an ongoing journey of learning from oneself and others, without fear or suffering, in both joyous and challenging trials.

In this regard, I'm deeply grateful to everyone who has helped me reach this point, allowing me to continue honoring this growth with fewer and fewer inner demons."

## Luke: "I remember my struggles in school because I didn't conform to the norms of the National Education system."

"Hello. I believe I might be an Indigo and/or Highly Gifted (HG)—what a dilemma! I exhibit most of the traits. I recall my school struggles because I didn't fit the patterns of the National Education system. There was always this sense of being different, of being misunderstood, even at work or in my reasoning. I've also experienced phenomena that some would describe as paranormal. The more my son grows, the more I believe he is also Indigo and HG. It was while searching for answers for him that I discovered the existence of Indigo and HG individuals."

## Jessica: "Diagnosed with Attention Deficit Disorder in 2019, just like my eldest child."

"I came across this article while grappling with countless questions about understanding life on both an individual and global level. It feels like it describes me perfectly, right down to the mention of ADHD [Attention Deficit Hyperactivity Disorder], which I was diagnosed with in 2019 (not detected during childhood thanks to strong compensatory skills). Additionally, my eldest child, who is 7 years old, received the same diagnosis. The question is: what should I do with all of this now?"

## Alice: "Many traits resonate with me, like my instinctive reasoning, heightened sensitivity, and tendency to absorb energies."

"Hello, I don't claim to be an Indigo, but many of these traits seem to describe me, particularly the instinctive aspect of my reasoning, my heightened sensitivity, and my general tendency to absorb energies. I also struggle with low self-esteem—several points resonate with me. But again, even if I feel different, I don't claim to be someone special."

## Chloe: "Heightened sensitivity, intuition, and ease of learning, but also significant difficulties with integration, despite my many skills and creativity."

"I was born in 1992 and believe I may be an Indigo. I've always felt different, even as a child, with a natural ease in expressing myself. I started speaking very early and quickly developed a passion for languages, music, and the arts, as well as an unconditional love for the stars and the sky. I've suffered from severe depression and extreme sensitivity, leading a life that has been turbulent, incredible, and unconventional, but also often magical.

I've faced my 'demons'—rejection from others, depression, psychiatric hospitalizations, school phobia, therapy, and completely extraordinary situations. Yet I've always maintained a strong 'connection,' acute intuition, déjà-vu experiences, flashes, premonitory dreams, and a great ability to understand others, perceive things, and feel others' emotions as if they were my own. I can grasp what people have been through, anticipate their reactions, or even predict what they will say.

I have an intense desire—almost a vital need—to help others, to contribute to improving life on this Earth, and an unwavering conviction that there is more, that extraordinary things are happening elsewhere. All this is accompanied by a deeply spiritual outlook. Yes, the life of an Indigo is not easy, but it is beautiful! We are unique, truly a big family at heart."

## Elisa: "An intense journey marked by profound suffering, but also extraordinary and magical experiences."

"Thank you for this truly fascinating article! I resonate with it deeply, as does my son! I was born in 1989, and he in 2006, and he strongly identifies with the description of an Indigo!

As for me, it's been—and still is—a very intense journey, full of suffering, but also extraordinary and magical!

I've just emerged from two and a half years of hardship (severe depression, or perhaps a spiritual awakening, burnout, leaving my job, a breakup after 12 years, illness, etc.), and what lies ahead is so extraordinary that I wouldn't trade this experience for anything, despite its challenges!"

## Emma: "Despite the challenges, I continue to remain open to others."

"I was born in 1977 and consider myself an Indigo. I fully identify with this description! I've always cared deeply for others, remaining a dreamer and often somewhat unrealistic. I always try to do my best, but in the end, everything seems to backfire. I've encountered many unkind people along my journey, likely because of my sensitivity. Nevertheless, I continue to remain open to others, even though this openness often leads to disappointment."

**Mia: "Heightened sensitivity, intuition, and learning ease, but challenges in integrating despite my many skills and creativity."**

"Everything resonates with me! I am an Indigo born in 1986. I've always felt different. I taught myself to read at the age of 4. From a young age, I've been highly sensitive, empathetic, intuitive, with premonitory dreams, déjà vu sensations, and an almost innate knowledge of what would happen.

I excelled academically but struggled socially with classroom bullies. I loved learning, particularly in artistic activities. By the age of 12, I spoke three languages and attended a school for intellectually gifted children.

Today, at 33, I speak six languages and hold a master's degree, but I still struggle to integrate, especially professionally, as I don't fit neatly into any 'box.'

Despite this, I've always excelled in everything I'm passionate about. My creativity and vibrant intelligence have unfortunately often sparked jealousy. I've made freer life choices, traveled, and nourished my spirituality, even when those around me didn't understand my path.

Sharing 33 years of life is no small feat, but I can say that this description represents me completely. To my fellow Indigos, I wish you all happiness."

**Anna: "Despite my numerous skills and heightened sensitivity, I've never managed to integrate socially or professionally, making my life painful and lonely."**

"Your description of Indigo adults matches me perfectly. This state has always been, and remains, a true curse for me.

I was born in 1973 and have always suffered because of these 'particular dispositions.' I've always been an outsider, both in school and the workplace.

I'm hyperactive, highly sensitive, and have been an insomniac my entire life. Some have even labeled me Asperger's. I speak several languages and have expertise in various fields, but despite this, I've never been able to integrate socially or professionally.

I haven't found a soulmate, nor do I have a family or children.

I am alone—not because I haven't met interesting people, but because none of them were suited to my personality. The few relationships I had ended badly.

Frankly, I wouldn't wish my experience on anyone, as it isolates me deeply from others and makes my life painful.

I'm 47 years old and still haven't found my true path. I feel like an alien in this world, in this era. I wonder where my soulmate is, if they even exist. What's the point of being here, on this earth, as an Indigo? I feel like an alien in the universal revelry."

## Mark: "Being an Indigo is a true blessing, always positive and a source of optimism, despite its complexity."

"Being an Indigo is a true blessing. Even though it's a complex condition, it is entirely positive. An Indigo cannot view their uniqueness as a curse. On the contrary, I reiterate—it's a blessing. An Indigo is naturally optimistic and strives for goodness, both in their own life and in the lives of others."

## Gabriel: "Suffering from heightened sensitivity and seasonal depression in Switzerland, I'm considering moving to a better climate after leaving my career as a dentist."

"I perfectly identify as an Indigo. At the moment, I'm suffering greatly due to my heightened sensitivity, particularly regarding the climate, which I can no longer tolerate here in Switzerland. I'm in a state of seasonal depression—it's terrible—but I'm considering relocating to a country with a better climate.

All my relationships have ended, and I haven't had children, but I feel I must follow my destiny. I'm 50 years old. I was a child prodigy in school and became a dentist, but I've left that profession. Now, I feel I need to find a new path."

## Julia: "Since childhood, I've always felt different. I've discovered my spirituality and deep intuitions, but I wonder if this explains my loneliness."

"I identify with many of the characteristics of Indigo children, even though I was born in 1964. I've always felt different, out of place since I was a child.

I've faced many challenges, both in my family and romantic life. For the past 10 years, thanks to my older sister, I've begun exploring another dimension of human existence.

I've learned a lot about personal development and spirituality through readings and 'mysterious' personal experiences. I've delved deep into myself and now know I'm not alone—I feel protected and guided. I often express gratitude for this richness that accompanies my earthly life.

I have many intuitions and perceptions, and at night I sense benevolent messages. However, what saddens me is not having friends or someone to share my life with. I wonder if this aspect of myself is the cause of my loneliness. Could that be the case?"

## Janet: "Now I feel completely fulfilled, happy, and capable of loving everyone around me without limits."

"I was born in 1953, and just yesterday, a shaman told me I'm an Indigo. Reading your article, I've gained a clearer understanding of my life. As the eldest of three siblings, I always struggled with the rules imposed by my parents, which made me unhappy. At 17, I was sent to France—a very difficult time. My parents saw me as an unbearable teenager. I'm originally from England.

Fortunately, I've always felt like I was on the right path, and since retiring, I've been working on myself—my thoughts and emotions. I'm learning to practice energy treatments.

My childhood seemed complicated, but now I feel completely fulfilled, happy, and capable of loving everyone around me without limits. I also want to add that working with energy helps me distinguish between emotions that come from others and those that belong to me."

## Agnes: "My childhood wasn't easy, marked by numerous conflicts."

"I recently attended a conference on cellular memory, where they also discussed Indigo children. It was suggested that I might be part of this group, even though I was born in 1957. After reading your article, I found myself in almost all of the 14 traits described.

It's true—my childhood wasn't easy, marked by many conflicts. I was always rebellious and naturally inclined to self-learning. Thank you for this information, which helps us better understand ourselves and work on our personal journeys."

## Rose: "I've learned to embrace my uniqueness, live with solitude (both within and around me), and love myself as an Indigo."

"I'm an Indigo born in 1972. From a young age, my father (who likely was an Indigo himself) always told me that I didn't fit in with others—whether in the family, at school, or elsewhere. I was 'different.' Even as a child, I felt like I didn't belong in this world.

Later, I told him I didn't recognize myself among the people around me. Around the age of 18, I freed myself from anything that could prevent me from being true to myself and existing as I truly am. I feel much closer to nature and animals, who help me recharge when I'm overwhelmed by the negativity around me.

I've learned to embrace my uniqueness, live with solitude (both internal and external), and most importantly, love myself as an Indigo. I don't seek anyone's recognition, nor do I expect others to love or 'accept' me for who I am. This is perhaps the price to pay for maintaining freedom.

This quest for freedom drives us to know and love ourselves so we're ready when the moment comes. I'm convinced there will come a time when we have a role to play in humanity, which is currently going through one of its most challenging phases of transformation. But first, we must undertake the journey of self-discovery—at least, that's my approach. It's a difficult path, but it works!

In any case, it's comforting to know we're not alone."

## Julius: "I've realized my life is a mission—not to teach with words but through my actions, leaving an imprint without any pretension of being better than others."

"I don't know what people born in 1953 are called! I just know I belong to the 'baby boomer' generation. From childhood, I've been extremely sensitive to my surroundings. Even at six or seven years old, I felt like I didn't belong in this world! I never thought like the people I knew and always felt distinct from society.

At 15, I rejected Catholicism, despite my parents' ultra-religious upbringing, and began a significant spiritual quest through reading. Then came the internet, with all its contradictions, but my intuition, inner guidance, and heart opened even further.

I've come to understand that my life is a mission—not to teach with words but through my actions, leaving an imprint behind me. Without any pretension of superiority, I have a deep desire to express what the Self (the God that I am, the God within me!) leads me to experience. I am nothing and yet I am you! And more often than I imagined, I discover that its will is even more beautiful than my initial personal desires.

Too often, I still find myself in judgment—of myself and others. I believe this is relatively normal, given my Judeo-Christian upbringing, where evil was seen everywhere... but I'm working on it. What initially was a quest for knowledge has become, over time, a quest to live and act better! In recent years, self-love has transformed into love for the Self, with growing love for others, especially those 'different' individuals who challenge us.

But it's not always easy. I remember reading that it's easy to love those who love us, but loving those who make us uncomfortable or who confront us with culturally different ways of living is another matter entirely.

All this to say that I identify with all 14 points—except the first. I was born long before 1978. As for point 10, where I admit I still eat too much meat, I recognize that I lack enough empathy for our animal brethren. If I had to kill a cow myself to eat my steak, I'd think twice!"

**Mary: "I've always felt different and now want to learn how to embrace this, turning it into a true strength rather than attracting negativity."**

"Finally, I can put a name to what I am... It's incredible how the comments and texts describe my experience perfectly.

I spent most of my school years almost entirely alone and have always felt this sense of being different. I thought it might be connected to my mother considering abortion and my father's psychological illness, which drove me to understand him without words.

But this is just a complement to who I am. Perhaps it even pushed me to be even more like this... so much suffering. I feel like I only surround myself with people who wish me harm or who can't give me what I need. I can't seem to break out of this pattern and truly be happy... I attract jealousy and competition, and in the end, I isolate myself to avoid problems.

Now here I am, at 1:16 in the morning, unable to sleep, reading your article, and I thank you! It resolves an existential doubt for me. I want to learn how to embrace this condition and turn it into a true strength rather than attracting negativity."

**Ryan: "I see myself in this, which reassures me about my nonconformity and resistance to rules and regulations, but I wonder how to use this awareness."**

"I do a lot of research online, but I find it very difficult to find my place in this world, or even to understand what use I could serve. I'm very interested in empaths and highly sensitive people because I see myself in all their traits.

I consider myself a multipotentialite, even though I've never taken the WAIS-IV test [Wechsler Adult Intelligence Scale], which I'm not particularly interested in due to its contested reliability. However, matching myself against the fourteen criteria I found online, I realized I identify with thirteen of them—I was born in 1973.

This reassures me, knowing I'm not the only nonconformist or the only one resistant to rules and regulations. Could I be an Indigo adult? And what could I do with this awareness if that's the case? It's truly overwhelming. Thank you."

**Steven: "I observe signs and synchronicities, feel accompanied, but suffer from not finding my place or someone who truly understands me."**

"I'm an Indigo. I see signs and synchronicities. The universe responds to me, and I feel accompanied. I receive messages through synchronicities, sometimes in dreams. I'm drawn to the sky and the stars.

I'm an emotional and empathetic sponge, but I'm often disappointed by people. I feel misunderstood, which leads to a loss of self-confidence. I have a strong sense of logic and reason. I put heart and love into everything I do, but I struggle here.

I need to love. I can't find my place or someone who truly resonates with me, and it's a source of pain."

**Leonard: "I've learned to embrace my uniqueness by freeing myself from the judgment of others and finding the courage to be myself."**

"I was born before 1978, but I identify 100% with the traits described. While it wasn't always easy when I was younger, I've learned to embrace my uniqueness. However, to do so, you have to free yourself from the weight of others' judgments and find the courage to live authentically, as you truly are."

**Hannah: "I've always felt different, despite the limited answers I received from my mother, who simply wanted me to discover it for myself by sending signals I never understood."**

"I stumbled across your article by chance, and I have to admit it provided me with many answers. I've always felt different, as if no one could understand me, let alone my way of thinking. Over the past two years, I've desperately sought answers from my mother.

She's very open to this universe, practices energy healing, and has ancestors who were druids. She knows a lot about these topics but has always avoided my questions. After reading your article, I slept poorly for two nights, driven by an incessant desire for answers. Finally, I called my mother and asked if she knew anyone who could see auras, and she told me that she could.

It was very difficult to get answers. I described to her what being an Indigo child means, and she already knew. In the end, she confessed that she had known since my birth but wanted me to discover it on my own, sending me signals that I never understood.

Despite these revelations, I know I won't get many more answers from her. So, I'll have to learn much on my own. But I thank you from the bottom of my heart because, for a long time, I felt almost crazy. Even during psychotherapy sessions and therapy groups in my teenage years, no one understood why I was so 'explosive' at times, or why I felt such an aversion to school in high school. Now I feel like I can finally understand and learn more about who I am. Thank you so much for your article."

## Paul: "I feel suffocated, misunderstood, and increasingly detached from society, as if I'm from another world."

"You know, I found in this article all the traits that describe me. I always feel like I have to hide who I really am. I don't suffer from depression, but I live with constant anxiety. I see things that will happen—things that are obvious to me. But if I try to talk about it, believe me, I'm rarely taken seriously.

People tell me to stop anticipating, to stop overthinking, to stop expecting the worst... Yet, in the end, those things do happen.

The worst decision I made to try to escape this inner discomfort about life and the way the world works was seeking help from a social worker. It was the biggest mistake of my life.

As soon as I entered the system, I felt suffocated, judged, and labeled. I never should have done it. It's difficult to feel what these people who are supposed to help you truly think. I see it in their eyes; I feel it clearly. And I know I'm not far from the truth.

How can I get out of this? It's hard for me to fit into their way of thinking. So, I pretend, and it makes me feel even more alone. The more time passes, the more distant I feel. I have the impression of being from another place.

My intuition is so strong. I can feel others' pain, no matter who they are, from far away, and it hits me deeply. More and more, I feel like everything around us—society, unconscious people—is unreal... Is this normal?"

**Roman: "I feel as if I've taken the red pill, awakened to a different reality, but freeing my true self remains a challenge."**

"Reading your work, I see myself in many of the points. I can't accept authority when it seems senseless. I'm a dreamer, highly empathetic, and I perceive my surroundings intensely. I'm nonconformist, and money or material possessions are not my priorities.

Right now, I'm working on myself, and I feel like I'm in 'The Matrix,' as if I've taken the red pill. It's incredible to realize how no one else seems to see the world the way I do. We're all conditioned from childhood!

I'm trying to free my soul—that part of me that is pure and untainted by the outside world. Every gesture, every thought is influenced by our conditioning. When I look inside myself and see beyond this false personality we're forced to show—and eventually believe is innate—I'm left speechless. What's inside me is so beautiful, so right, so immense!

I strive to let my true self, my dormant soul, emerge, but it's difficult. It's so easy to give in to the temptation to follow the crowd and live like everyone else! A few months ago, I had a vision, like a painting, where I could see all the paths of my life. I found many answers about the world around us and understood everything.

That moment was very intense and triggered something within me, like a wake-up call. It was then that I understood which path to take and what my role is! But first, I must work on myself, to understand myself better, to truly know myself—and that's not easy!"

**Hugh: "I sense others' emotions, which is frustrating but helps me manage situations better."**

"I identify with nine out of the fourteen traits mentioned, including my birth date and my sleep disturbances. People often tell me I'm very wise and resilient. However, a few years ago, I discovered that I can perceive others' emotions.

For example, I can tell if my partner is sad or in pain, and I feel those negative emotions myself. It's frustrating to constantly absorb such feelings, and I haven't yet found a way to block this phenomenon.

That said, this ability helps me manage situations better because it allows me to deeply understand what others are going through and act with greater awareness."

### Genevieve: "Sensitivity, empathy, and a different vision of the world that enriches diversity."

"Thank you for this article! I resonate completely: sensitivity, strong empathy, and that sense of having a 'mission.' I have the ability to see what others don't, to pick up on subtle behaviors.

Born in 1989, I don't seek to define myself as 'different,' but rather to name what sets me apart. I don't claim to be superior—simply to see the world differently. Diversity is what makes this world rich and unique."

### Louis: "Going through a tough time facing humanity's resistance to evolve: accepting oneself and choosing love is key to our well-being."

"I felt the need to write you a few words. Even though I don't like labels, I identify with what you describe.

Lately, I've faced very difficult moments. I've always promoted love, but I constantly clash with humanity's resistance to evolve, and it deeply discourages me.

I've felt anger and rejection toward humanity, thinking that everything could be simpler if each person decided to overcome their fears and beliefs.

Born in 1988, your article helped me recentralize: accepting oneself and living in love, adapting to a different way of functioning, is the key to our well-being.

It's important to preserve what we feel. This emanation of my being, which surpasses me, must be protected—even if I sometimes struggle to recognize what others perceive as a strong inner light."

**Benjamin: "Discovering that Indigo characteristics reflect my life path, marked by a perceived difference since childhood, makes me eager to explore this topic further."**

"I was born in 1964 and had no idea about Indigo children until now. I'm amazed by how many aspects of their description align with my life, even from childhood—though I don't consider anything an absolute truth.

A visit to a psychologist at age 8 confirmed I had a high IQ, coupled with behavior that didn't match my age. I struggled in 'standard' schools but thrived in alternative ones I chose for myself.

People have given me nicknames like 'alien,' 'guardian angel,' 'healer,' and 'seer with golden hands.' I've always been drawn to esotericism and spirituality.

I'm often described as reactionary and nonconformist, feeling the constant need to reinvent the world over and over again. I break everything down into its components to analyze it individually. Identifying with a single term like this is both interesting and, honestly, reassuring.

Thank you—I'm inspired to delve deeper into this subject."

**Sophia: "Born in 1956, I identify as an Indigo. I've experienced profound spiritual moments, often misunderstood, leaving me feeling isolated despite the support of those around me."**

"I am undoubtedly an Indigo, even though I was born in 1956. I've identified at least ten past lives and observed many strange coincidences and premonitions that manifest through flashes, dreams, or even songs. Sometimes, I even find jewelry on the ground that carries deep meaning during pivotal moments in my life.

It's not easy, and people often see us as aliens (I'm frequently told I look 20 years younger than my age). I often feel depressed because, despite the support of family and friends, I have a profound sense of loneliness.

I've fallen in love twice with men I had intense relationships with in past lives. But the issue is that 'normal' men don't understand these experiences. I could enter their minds, and astonishing coincidences would occur, yet these relationships never materialized in the earthly realm."

**Mark: "Born in 1967, I've always felt different, driving me to explore spiritual practices to understand myself and overcome life's challenges. Now, I see spiritual awakening as essential for humanity's elevation and universal balance."**

"Apart from not seeing auras or identifying geometric shapes in food, everything you described matches me. I was born in January 1967, and at 20, during a military service assessment, they discovered my IQ was 140. This explained a lot—I've always felt different. The only subjects that interested me were arts, French, applied mathematics, and natural and physical sciences. Today, quantum physics fascinates me because it bridges ancient wisdom and science, offering a broader and integrated vision of life and creation.

I've never tolerated authority and often mocked those exercising it, causing laughter even in the military, which, of course, created problems. Over the years, I endured painful events and had a harsh mother, filling me with anger and resentment. However, I began a healing journey using various tools: meditation, shamanism, family constellations, and reading works like The Power of Now by Eckhart Tolle and The Four Agreements by Don Miguel Ruiz. These paths inflated my spiritual ego, but I wasn't yet embodying what I learned.

Three years ago, during a workshop on emotional management and shamanism, a holistic doctor told me I had great potential as a healer and teacher. This profoundly shifted my perspective. I've worked intensely on myself and met people who've helped me accept myself and find greater peace, though traumatic memories still surface occasionally.

A numerologist friend explained that my life mission is to contribute to the emergence of a new planetary consciousness. This gave me a renewed sense of purpose, even in a society quick to label people as 'bipolar' or 'nonconformist,' which I've always found limiting.

Through meditation, astral journeys, and self-work, I'm

learning detachment and letting go—one of life's greatest challenges, I believe. We are living through an era of immense energetic transformation, calling humanity to awaken and contribute to Gaia's ascension and universal balance. Despite the chaos, many are awakening, raising vibrations, and transforming our planet.

I believe each of us plays a role in this process. The true challenge is to heal our wounds, transcend duality, and reclaim our true nature as multidimensional, limitless, and eternal beings of light, in harmony with the whole. This is humanity's most crucial moment—a unique opportunity for transformation for ourselves and the universe."

**Jade: "I consider myself an Indigo, searching for meaning since my awakening in May 2016. Although it destabilizes me at times, I'm determined to find balance and better understand my path."**

"Thank you so much for your beautiful words. It's always comforting to know you're not alone. I consider myself an Indigo, trying every day to find my way, even though I sometimes feel adrift. I believe my daughter is an Indigo too, and I do my best to support her. We're both highly sensitive, especially during the full moon!

I began awakening in May 2016, and since then, I've often had dreams whose meanings I don't understand. This sometimes unsettles me even more. I'm trying to hold on as best I can."

**Victor: "At 17, I feel exhausted by others' emotions. It prevents me from fully living, leaving me constantly drained, and despite my efforts, I can't find a solution."**

"This article doesn't fully apply to me since I'm only 17, but I've experienced this since childhood. For years, people around me have considered me strange or assumed I'd be diagnosed as bipolar in the future. Everything described fits me perfectly and keeps me from truly living. Being around others tires me because I constantly feel their anger, their fear... These emotions trigger crises that I often take out on my family.

I'm still in school, but nothing excites me—I'm terribly bored.

I'm always tired, sleep poorly, and wake up panicked. I've seen a psychologist who said she'd prescribe me antidepressants if I were an adult. The thing is, nothing sad has happened in my life. I just don't know how to handle these emotions, and people end up distancing themselves from me.

Now, I can tell when I'm beginning to feel others' emotions—I get stomachaches and sometimes nausea. Honestly, I don't find anything positive about this. I've tried managing it, but nothing seems to work."

**David: "At 46, I see myself in the characteristics of Indigos, particularly through my unique visual experiences and rejection of conventional systems, though this often leaves me feeling isolated and misunderstood."**

"I don't know where to start because, at 46, born in 1971, my life has been full of varied experiences, and I also pursue parallel reflective projects. I identify perfectly with the 14 traits mentioned in your article—perhaps even more.

For years now, I've experienced something unique that began around age 25. I see color spectrums on certain objects or people. At first, it unsettled me, and I'd rub my eyes, but nothing changed. So, I thought, 'I must have an eye problem—I should see a specialist.'

The results were surprising: yes, I have an eye condition, but not one that affects my vision negatively. My eyes are overly sensitive to light, often tearing up, especially in dim settings. The specialist made me custom sunglasses, calling my condition rare and, in a way, fortunate. For me, it was more of an annoyance than anything else.

Once I got the glasses, I was happy to have light protection, but the light spectrums continued to appear in my peripheral vision. When I went back to the specialist, he told me there was nothing abnormal about my eyes and that my vision was excellent. He explained that there was nothing else he could do.

Feeling disappointed, I learned to live with it. The phenomenon doesn't happen constantly, but it occurs at least once a week, as far back as I can remember.

Another aspect of me is my rebellious nature: I strongly believe our systems aren't suited for the uncontrolled demographic growth across continents. I lead integration projects and feel deeply skeptical about imposed rules. I also have a fascination with prime numbers, which I've been studying for nearly 12 years.

In dreams, I see geometric patterns that won't let me sleep until I sketch them out. I work meticulously, adhering to principles like 1.618, the golden ratio.

I could keep writing, but I'd risk turning this into a novel. There's no need to add more, as I have too much to say. Still, I'm unsure if I'm truly an Indigo. One thing is certain: I often feel alone because I quickly grow bored with people who don't understand me. Thank you for your article—I stumbled upon it entirely by chance."

**Matthew: "This week, I've been discovering my ties to empathy and Indigo traits, finding explanations for my behavior, even though I don't fully align with all the criteria."**

"So many discoveries this week...
I don't fully agree with the 'irrational' aspect. First, I learned about my ties to empaths, which led me to Indigos. I found many explanations for my reactions and ways of being—plenty of answers.

I don't share every commonality: I was born in 1966, and for point 10, I don't align at all. Aside from that, everything fits perfectly.

I could say so much more, but thank you for introducing me to all of this. I'll explore the topic further, though I believe the reasons behind our presence may have a hidden dimension."

**Olivia: "After confirming my Indigo identity, I feel more at peace and determined to follow my intuition, contributing—even modestly—to the world's evolution."**

"Yes, here I am. I was born in 1973. I intuitively felt that I belonged to this dimension, and two years ago, a Reiki master confirmed it for me. I knew I was Indigo but didn't fully understand what it meant. Now, I feel more at peace knowing what Indigos are meant to do.

I'm more resolute in my outlook and no longer disheartened by opposing opinions. My intuition is right—I feel it within me. In my own small way, I challenge the system. I contribute to the world's evolution, no matter how modest my role may be.

Thank you for this article, and I send a ray of light to my Indigo brothers and sisters."

**Chloe: "As an Indigo adult, empathic and hypersensitive, I often feel overwhelmed by emotions, especially after a motorcycle accident in 2005. I'm seeking advice on managing this intensity and potential better."**

"I am an Indigo adult, but that's not all. It's part of me, but I am also an empath and hypersensitive. I don't understand this world; I often say it's not mine. Authority and I are incompatible. I love feeling free in everything I do.

Being an Indigo, hypersensitive, and empathic in today's world is really difficult. I only recently came to understand this, following a life event—a motorcycle accident in 2005. I was in a coma for three weeks. When I woke up, I was different.

I experienced a profound emotional shock, and since then, I approach everything with extremes. It's difficult because I don't realize it at the moment.

I won't go on too long, but I'd love to know how to harness this potential and manage all these emotions that tend to overwhelm me."

**Olivia: "Since childhood, I've felt different and connected to paranormal experiences, leading me to explore parapsychology and discover my Indigo identity, which I share with several generations of my family."**

"Answering 'yes' to all the questions, and adding that as a child, I was sure I came from another place, I've always felt different. Born in 1952, people back then considered me 'strange.'

After my great-grandmother's death, she guided me to books that revealed who I was. For the first time, I was happy to put a name to my paranormal experiences and moments of isolation, as it was impossible to explain what was happening back then.

Moving objects, the scents of deceased relatives, voices offering help, premonitory dreams, and visions led me to explore parapsychology for over 40 years.

I worked with dowsing rods, pendulums, tarot cards, and numerology, all confirming the existence of another world on a different plane guiding us.

For years, when turning off the lights to sleep, I would see faces of unknown people flashing quickly before me, too fast to focus on. Later, I began seeing luminous geometric shapes, glowing blue spheres, and lavender-colored pyramids. I tried to grab them, but it was impossible.

My room's night background resembled the universe: everything moved with white lights and more. There's still much to share—this is just a glimpse of my experiences.

Today, thanks to the internet and serendipitous encounters, I can talk more freely about what is normal for me, even if science can't explain it. I've had many extrasensory experiences with witnesses, reassuring me they weren't imaginary or signs of schizophrenia, thank goodness!

I have O-negative blood, green eyes, light brown hair, and have always felt from another world. I had a vision of black-clad beings with elongated heads, hoods, and gloves looking at me over a large crater-like opening, discussing among themselves.

This is just part of who I am, now identified as an Indigo. Interestingly, my children, grandchildren, mother, and great-grandmother share this trait, forming quite a group. Thank you for exploring this Indigo and paranormal realm—it's comforting to read about others rooted in the same reality."

**Sophia: "After realizing I am an Indigo and overcoming confusion between my emotions and others', I feel reborn, finding my element as a magnetizer and NLP practitioner."**

"Hello, I am indeed an Indigo. I wasn't sure at first, but I align with the points described in the article, except for the emotional absorption, which I stopped experiencing recently.

Previously, I would confuse my emotions with others', leading to depression—until my life changed entirely. At that moment, I truly felt reborn.

This is my first time leaving a comment. Thank you for your page—it covers everything I'm interested in.

I am a magnetizer and have started practicing NLP with others, so I feel completely in my element reading your blog. Thank you!"

**Mia: "As an Indigo hypersensitive to others' energies, I've struggled with a lack of protective barriers, and I'm happy to have found your site to better understand and manage this sensitivity.**

"I see myself in the description of Indigo personalities, even though I was born in 1972. I am hypersensitive and feel like I absorb all the energies of people and places.

This has become a problem in recent months, as it's as if I no longer have any protective barriers—I feel completely permeable.

So far, I haven't sought ways to protect myself, but I'm glad I found your site and will read your articles carefully. Thank you!"

**Charlotte: "As an Indigo, I suffer from hypersensitivity and a sense of estrangement from this world, which often leads me to isolate myself. I wonder if others share this feeling."**

"I identify with all 14 traits... and have suffered a lot because of them. I think I'm an Indigo, and I see this in my children, especially my daughter. Hypersensitivity is the hardest to manage, along with not understanding a world that often feels so alien to me.

I tend to isolate myself because I absorb others' suffering—sometimes, I cry just looking at someone. I used to think I was just overly empathetic and sensitive... I always asked myself many questions.

I believe I've found answers, but I feel deep down that the cause is lost... that this world is lost. Am I the only one who feels this way?"

**Elizabeth: "I identify as a young Indigo adult, grappling with emotional disturbances and deeply absorbing others' emotions while developing a greater understanding of the spiritual mechanism surrounding us."**

"This isn't the first time someone has told me, and after researching and reading your article, I've confirmed that I am a young Indigo adult.

Born in 1994, I've always struggled in school and with relationships. My mother took me to see many psychologists, and I was prescribed Ritalin for my attention disorder.

Today, I live with a diagnosis of bipolar disorder, predominantly depressive. I suffer from anxiety and depression, experiencing my emotions and those of others with a depth that can sometimes overwhelm me.

The further I progress in life, the more I understand the spiritual mechanism around us. Thank you."

**Lauren: "Born in 1973, I am an 'emotional sponge,' seeking balance between my artistic talents and rational side. Despite professional successes, I often doubt myself and continue searching for equilibrium."**

"Born in 1973, someone I met professionally made me aware of this trait: I am an emotional sponge, anxious, capable of being both highly artistic and rational (I am an engineer).

Since childhood, I conformed to others because I sensed my differences unsettled them. Fortunately, my parents had an intuitive understanding of my nature, even though they didn't know about Indigo theories. They told me I was maternal with my classmates—a real Saint Bernard!

Only now am I beginning to come to terms with this reality. I've returned to herbalism studies, but I still struggle with the fact that I often work faster than my colleagues, manage everything, know so much, and appear super confident, even though I'm constantly doubting myself!

There's still a long way to go... Perhaps coaching could help? In any case, it's such a joy to read your article! Thank you."

## Liam: "I believe our mission on Earth is spiritual evolution—accepting our hypersensitivity and guiding others toward pure love as we grow closer to this evolution with each reincarnation."

"Here's what I think: we are all here for a good reason. Each reincarnation leads us to experiences we offer to God, who shares them with us. We are never alone; we are always accompanied.

Some souls, still young and with low energy, are unaware of the awakening happening. Thankfully, for millennia, reincarnated guides have accompanied us with love.

For those who feel their differences, they are the most 'normal.' We must repay our debts, from which our hypersensitivity stems. Accepting this allows us to progress.

I was born in 1978, but the year doesn't matter because beings have awaited evolution for millennia. Why are some of us disturbed by what the world offers today? It's because God gave us free will, and over time, we've often misused it.

It's up to us—the awakened—to show the way and help others toward the ultimate evolution: pure love."

## Angelina: "Born in 1974, I identify with many Indigo traits, and through Reiki training, I'm reconnecting with my true inner self and life mission."

"I identify with most of the traits described in your article: boredom in school, hypersensitivity, rebellion, intolerance of authority, anxiety...

My intuition is highly developed, and I often feel out of place. Born in 1974, I've only recently started reclaiming my personal power.

I began training as a Reiki practitioner, which is helping me reconnect with my true inner self and life mission. Thank you for this beautiful article."

**Ava: "Born in 1986, I've often been misunderstood for perceiving the colors of people, but learning that I am Indigo has helped me understand myself better."**

"Born in 1986, people thought I was crazy when I explained that each person has a color I can perceive... Now I know they were the ones who didn't understand anything.

The 14 traits described align perfectly with who I am. Thank you for shedding light on this topic."

**Charlotte: "At 25, I identify as Indigo, nonconformist but not militant, preferring to pave new paths and share my vision of a meaningful life without imposing it on others."**

"I am officially a 25-year-old Indigo adult!

Predefined paths have never been for me, and I often feel like the world works in reverse. One thing puzzles me: I thought Indigos were rebels openly fighting against society—militants whose sole aim was to awaken consciousness and restructure existing systems.

I am fundamentally nonconformist and rarely follow the crowd. My choices often go against the grain of the majority.

However, I am not always fighting against something. Instead, I pave new paths for those ready to walk them.

In short, I am different from others and desire societal evolution to help people feel more fulfilled, but I don't impose my vision on others. I simply share it, showing that it's possible to live a happy and meaningful life. Congratulations on the article, and thank you!"

**Abigail: "At 45, I see myself as Indigo, using my empathy and sensitivity to help others as a palliative care nurse. I believe we are souls having a human experience."**

"I am 45 and identify as Indigo; my daughter is as well.

I've always felt different and wanted to change things. I am an artist and only create when guided by intuition or when I intuitively feel the need to make something.

I deeply feel others' energy, which helps me in my work as a palliative care nurse, where my strengths lie in empathy, accompanying patients through death, and supporting grieving families.

I have the ability to absorb another person's energy and channel it, reduce it, or even transmit some of mine.

I consider myself a messenger. I am very open-minded and believe we are souls having a human experience on Earth.

Thank you for this article and for everything you publish— it's truly inspiring and thought-provoking."

**Lily: "Your article confirms that I am an adult Indigo, having always felt deeply different and unstable due to my heightened curiosity, which made self-acceptance a challenge until now."**

"Good morning.

Thank you for your article, which once again confirms that I am an adult Indigo. Born in 1980, I've always felt different from others, whether with my parents or at school.

Work life has always been a nightmare for me because of authority... I've always felt faster than others, and for a long time, I saw this trait as a flaw until I learned to accept myself for who I am.

I've always lived in a state of constant instability due to my excessive curiosity... Thank you for giving this phenomenon a name."

**Grace: "As an Indigo, I feel profoundly different and at odds with the world, driven by a strong sense of empathy and justice, yet often misunderstood despite my desire to help others."**

"I've always felt different, and for several years now, I've known I'm an Indigo.

As a child, I already asked existential questions that aren't typically asked at such a young age, like why life on Earth isn't longer, why we die, and I also had the impression that I wasn't alone.

I still feel all of this today and continue to perceive myself as different, out of sync with the world as it is. I rarely agree with others—except with the Indigos I feel around me.

I have too much empathy for others and an acute sense of right and wrong.

I try to maintain positive thoughts and spend a lot of time dispelling the negative ones, but it's exhausting, and I often feel like I'm swimming against the current.

I've always believed I was born to help others, but I am misunderstood. Oh well, I'll keep going anyway."

**Amelia: "As an empathetic Indigo, I've discovered with frustration that my ability to heal others leaves me physically and emotionally drained, as I didn't realize the profound impact of others' energy on my body."**

"I was born in 1986, and I am 1000% an Indigo and empathetic, but I can't take it anymore!

I'm a therapist with all the possible knowledge—except one…

No one ever told me that you can be confident, trust your abilities, and know how to say no or stop while still absorbing all the difficult energies of others into your body without even realizing it.

This absorption has brought me to the point of wanting to leave this Earth due to intense inner and physical exhaustion, with no apparent material cause.

So, I looked inward and discovered that I wanted to 'redeem my past mistakes' by alleviating others' suffering.

I had forgotten to tell the Universe: not at my expense! And I had no awareness of absorbing all this into my body."

And now, let these stories resonate within you, like an echo reminding you that you are never truly alone.

Perhaps you've found fragments of yourself in each of these accounts—reflections of your experiences and emotions. These stories, though deeply personal, weave a common thread that connects us all. They remind you that, even in your most isolated moments, there is a community of souls sharing your journey, your questions, and your hopes.

Allow yourself to feel this profound connection, to remember that these voices, scattered across the world, come together in a collective murmur of support and understanding. It is no coincidence that you have encountered these stories, and it is no coincidence that you continue to move forward. Every word you've read, every emotion you've felt, is part of a greater journey—a journey in which you are never truly alone.

Together, share this inner light with others, this quiet strength that drives you to seek, to understand, and to grow. Through these pages, you have touched the reality that you are one with a community of Indigo souls united by a shared quest for meaning and truth.

And as you continue on your journey, remember that this connection will always be with you, wherever you are and whatever you do. Together, you journey forward, guided by a simple yet profound truth:

**"You are never alone, and you never will be."**

# 8 SYNCHRONICITY: THE SPIRITUAL NAVIGATION SYSTEM OF THE INDIGO SOULS

*"Synchronicity is an ever-present reality for those who have eyes to see."* — Carl Gustav Jung

*"The only journey is the one within."* — Rainer Maria Rilke

*"Knowing yourself is the beginning of all wisdom."* — Aristotle

Let me share with you a phenomenon that often arises when embarking on the journey of self-discovery, something you have likely encountered as you began exploring the concept of Indigo adults. I'm referring to synchronicity—that mysterious convergence where two events align perfectly, without any apparent connection, yet their meeting awakens profound meaning in the observer. As always, I will recount this through my own personal experience.

Years had passed. I was living in another city, in another country. I found myself in the southwest of the United Kingdom, in a tiny village nestled in the English countryside.

That day, I was at the foot of Glastonbury Tor. This iconic hill in Somerset, England, is crowned by St. Michael's Tower, the remains of a medieval church dedicated to Saint Michael. This mystical site is steeped in legends and mythology, making it a focal point of spirituality and British folklore.

From a mythical perspective, the Tor is often linked to Avalon, the legendary island tied to the Arthurian cycle, where it is said King Arthur was taken to heal after his final battle. Other traditions regard it as one of the gateways to the fairy realm or a sacred site for druids—the ancient Celtic priests I have spoken about before. Glastonbury Tor stands as a crossroads of myth, nature, and spirit, and on that day, I experienced firsthand how synchronicity could illuminate the path toward greater self-understanding.

Its position and natural terraced structure have long inspired speculation about the ritual use of the Tor, perhaps as a pagan ceremonial center. The mystical energy that many visitors claim to feel is commonly associated with ley lines—energy paths believed to crisscross the British landscape, connecting various sacred sites.

I began my ascent, step by step, drawing closer to the summit and sensing the ancient energy of the place. The wind carried whispers of centuries past, and upon reaching the top, I gazed at the endless expanse of green hills. Up there, I felt a profound connection, as if that sacred site was reminding me of my place in a greater whole—rooted in time and space and bound to the Earth's most ancient energies.

Nestled within the mystical landscape of Glastonbury is the Sacred Spring, known as the White Spring, a site steeped in history and legend. This ancient source has long been revered as a powerful wellspring of healing and spiritual renewal. It is said that the waters of the White Spring carry the energies of the Earth's deepest wells, connecting those who seek them to the primordial forces of nature.

The uniqueness of this water lies in its iron-rich composition, which gives it a taste reminiscent of blood. This characteristic, known and revered since ancient times, has cemented its symbolism of life, sacrifice, and regeneration. To the Celts, these waters were sacred, believed to be blessed by the gods and imbued with the power to purify, heal, and transform.

Standing by the spring, I could feel the weight of its legacy—a convergence of myth, nature, and spirit that invited me to reflect on the timeless cycles of life and renewal. It was as though the energy of the place whispered ancient truths, reminding me of the interconnectedness of all things.

Its unique properties and deep connection to the Earth continue to draw those seeking spiritual answers and a bond with the eternal forces of nature. The spring has witnessed countless pilgrims, from ancient Druids to modern seekers, captivated by the promise of communion with the divine. People gather here not only to drink or bathe in its waters but also to honor the ancient rites of their ancestors. They light candles, offer prayers, and feel the presence of those who came before—the Celts, who revered these waters as a manifestation of life itself.

The White Spring is often described as a channel, a place where the veil between worlds is thin, allowing the Earth's energies to intertwine with those who seek them. Many visitors, drawn by the unique energy of this site, come for spiritual practices or meditation. Among them are numerous followers of Wicca, a modern pagan religion inspired by ancient beliefs.

Wicca emphasizes harmony with nature, reverence for the cycles of life, and the balance between the sacred masculine and feminine. Practitioners celebrate solstices, equinoxes, and the phases of the moon, performing rituals that honor natural elements, pagan deities, and the spirits of the natural world.

That day, however, I felt the urge to retreat to the sanctuary of my home, craving solitude. Sometimes I need time for myself, and this was one of those times.

***"Why was I so drawn to the Indigo people, and what role was I meant to play?"*** I pondered.

Sunlight gently streamed into my apartment, illuminating every corner with a soft, comforting glow. I noticed how much care I had put into creating a warm and inviting space: lush green plants thrived in every corner, and bookshelves brimmed with knowledge.

The harmony of the room was captivating. Shades of beige mingled with the vibrant greens of the foliage, forming a living, energizing tableau. The space exuded a unique serenity, an enchanting interplay of light and shadow that seemed almost alive.

Yet I felt lost. I kept uncovering more about Indigo people, but ***"what did it all mean? What was I supposed to do with this knowledge? Should I let it go and return to other pursuits?"*** I longed for signs to help me understand my path.

As I sat in contemplation, the radio played softly in the background, something I wasn't paying much attention to—until a melody suddenly captured my senses, like a gentle awakening. It was an Italian song, its evocative sound transporting me elsewhere. On British radio, such a song was unusual. I was certain it carried a message for me.

The song was Gli Uccelli by Franco Battiato, a symphony that transcends space and time[4].

It filled the space with evocative sounds, resonating deeply within me.

The poetic and mystical tones of the music acted as a catalyst, sparking a sudden realization, a revelation that began to take shape in my mind.

I quickly jotted down the words I managed to capture in the moment and began to research them further.

As soon as I had the chance to read the full lyrics, I was profoundly moved.

With each line unveiled, the words became a gateway to a world of emotions and reflections. To me, it was unmistakable—it was speaking

---

[4] Franco Battiato, an Italian multidisciplinary artist, distinguished himself through his unique talent, transcending artistic boundaries to explore profound spiritual horizons. Born on March 23, 1945, in Sicily, Battiato left an indelible mark on both the Italian and international art scenes as a singer, composer, filmmaker, and writer.

His musical career, which began in the 1960s, evolved over time to encompass a wide array of styles, from pop to experimental rock and electronic music. What truly sets Battiato apart, however, is his fearless exploration of spiritual and metaphysical themes through music and lyrics.

Battiato was not just an artist but a spiritual seeker who used art as his medium. His quest for meaning led him to weave elements of Eastern philosophy, esotericism, and spirituality into his work. The lyrics of his songs reveal profound reflections on the nature of existence, the awakening of consciousness, and the continuous search for inner truth.

His iconic album Fetus (1972) marked the beginning of his deeper exploration of spiritual themes. Tracks like La Cura (The Cure) and L'Ombra della Luce (The Shadow of the Light) combine mystical influences with innovative musical arrangements. As a musical alchemist, Battiato blended sounds and ideas to create a sensory experience that transcends mere entertainment.

In parallel with his musical career, Battiato ventured into the world of cinema, directing films such as Perduto Amor (Lost Love, 2003). His cinematic works often mirrored his spiritual concerns, delving into the nature of reality, consciousness, and transcendence.

Franco Battiato was far more than a musician. He embodied the essence of a visionary artist, a poet of sound probing the depths of the human soul in search of metaphysical answers. His music, imbued with timeless spirituality, continues to inspire and awaken consciousness, inviting audiences on an inner journey that surpasses the conventional boundaries of musical art.

about the Indigo.

"Birds fly, they fly
Through the space between the clouds
With the rules assigned
To this part of the universe
To our solar system.
They spread their wings,
Dive swiftly, land
Better than airplanes,
They change the world's perspectives.
Unpredictable flights and rapid ascents,
Imperceptible trajectories,
Codes of existential geometry.
Birds migrate, they emigrate
With the changing seasons,
Games of wing movements
That conceal the secrets
Of this solar system.
They spread their wings,
Dive swiftly, land
Better than airplanes,
They change the world's perspectives.
Unpredictable flights and rapid ascents,
Imperceptible trajectories,
Codes of existential geometry.
Birds fly, they fly
Through the space between the clouds
With the rules assigned

**To this part of the universe**
**To our solar system..."**

The simplicity of these words carries the weight of centuries, evoking a timeless sense of wisdom. As I delved deeper into the labyrinth of understanding Indigo adults, their essence remained elusive, much like the fleeting melody in Franco Battiato's song: mysterious, profound, and layered with meaning.

### 1. Universal Connection

The song speaks of birds flying through the space between clouds, following rules assigned to this part of the universe and our solar system. This cosmic perspective mirrors the Indigo people's deep connection to the universe and their sense of universal purpose. They often perceive patterns and energies that extend beyond the immediate physical realm.

### 2. Unconventional Perspectives

The lyrics highlight how birds change the world's perspectives with their unpredictable flights, rapid ascents, and imperceptible trajectories. Similarly, Indigo individuals are known for their unconventional thinking and visions. They frequently challenge societal norms and contribute fresh, innovative approaches to various aspects of life.

### 3. Migration and Transformation

The reference to birds migrating with the changing seasons resonates with the idea that Indigo adults often undergo profound personal and spiritual transformations. Like the migratory paths of birds, these individuals experience evolutionary shifts in consciousness, seek new horizons, and adapt to the ever-changing seasons of life.

### 4. Geometry of Existence

The mention of "codes of existential geometry" in the song reflects the notion that Indigo individuals have an innate understanding of complex patterns and subtle energies. This is evident in their ability to grasp deep interconnections, both in human relationships and within the broader context of existence.

### 5. Mysteries and Depth

The unfolding of birds' wings concealing the secrets of our solar system symbolizes the profound insight of Indigo people into life's mysteries. Their heightened intuition and spiritual awareness often lead them to uncover hidden truths that remain unseen by others.

### 6. Harmony with Nature

The overarching theme of the song, with birds soaring in the sky and following universal rules, evokes the sense of communion with nature frequently attributed to Indigo individuals. They often align with cosmic rhythms and experience synchronicities that guide their journey, living in harmony with the natural and spiritual worlds.

In summary, Gli Uccelli captures the essence of transformation and connection with the cosmos. It aligns with the traits often attributed to Indigo adults, who navigate life's complexities with a unique perspective and a profound sense of interconnectedness with the universe. The song becomes a metaphorical journey, mirroring the experiences and perceptions of those who resonate with the Indigo spirit.

As I walked into the kitchen to grab a glass of water, something impossible unfolded before my eyes: a small robin was desperately trying to escape through the kitchen's glass door. Trapped inside, it had somehow entered without explanation, as every window and door in the house had been securely closed. I stood in awe, recognizing this moment as a striking example of synchronicity.

Without hesitation, I freed the robin, which darted out through the glass door like a bolt of lightning. Before disappearing, it perched briefly on a plant in my small garden, turning toward me as if to offer a parting glance. Then it vanished forever, slipping back into the invisible realm from which it had emerged, just moments after it had so strikingly captured my attention.

In this moment of synchronicity—where time, space, and symbolism converge—signs like these become milestones, reassuring us that our path aligns with a greater design.

The concept of synchronicity, popularized by Swiss psychologist Carl Jung, intertwines profoundly with the fabric of our exploration. Jung defined synchronicity as a meaningful coincidence, a bridge between the inner world of individual psyche and the external world of objectivity.

According to Jung, synchronicities are signs that appear seemingly by chance yet carry both subjective and universal meaning.

Thus, the presence of the bird in my kitchen, aligned with the melody of Battiato's song, becomes a synchronicity: a convergence between internal experience and the external world. As Jung asserted, such events are not mere accidents but manifestations of a hidden order connecting the psychic and physical planes.

When we delve into synchronicities, we are invited to uncover the deeper significance of these chance encounters, to search for hidden patterns, and to recognize that these signs might guide us toward the right path.

It is in this dance—between the enigma of Indigo adults, synchronicities, and the timeless melody of Gli Uccelli—that a fascinating tapestry of my human experience and connection to the universe's mystery unfolded.

*"If this is a sign,"* I thought, *"then there must be a reason for my interest in Indigo individuals."*

I had to continue my search.

# 9 INDIGO CHILDREN: EMBRACING THE WISDOM OF SENSITIVE SOULS

*"There is no greater force than gentleness."* — Han Suyin

*"It is no measure of health to be well adjusted to a profoundly sick society."* — Jiddu Krishnamurti

*"Be yourself; everyone else is already taken."* — Oscar Wilde


At this point, you may have already realized whether you identify as an Indigo individual. If you have children, many of these traits might also resonate with your experience as the parent of an Indigo child.

Raising an Indigo child can be both profoundly rewarding and uniquely challenging. That's why this chapter is dedicated to such an important and delicate topic.

The upbringing of an Indigo child requires a careful balance of intuition, creativity, and a deep understanding of their unique spiritual and emotional needs. Sensitivity is not a weakness but a profound source of wisdom. Sensitive souls are not lost; they awaken to deeper realities.

First and foremost, Indigo children are characterized by their intuitive nature, overflowing creativity, and deep empathy for the world. They may often feel disconnected or misunderstood due to their heightened perceptions. However, it is crucial to recognize and nurture their extraordinary abilities.

By fostering an environment of understanding and support, you can help your child navigate a world that often feels misaligned with their sensibilities. They carry gifts meant to inspire transformation, and your role as a parent is to guide them in channeling these strengths while cultivating resilience and self-assurance.

Indigo children, often described as intuitive and uniquely gifted, are gaining increasing attention from parents and those passionate about spirituality.

During her research with children in the 1970s and 1980s, synesthete and psychotherapist Nancy Ann Tappe observed that some exhibited a dominant auric color: indigo.

If you're wondering whether your child might be an Indigo, here are some key traits that may help you identify them.

### 1. Advanced Sensitivity

Indigo children are deeply sensitive beings, acutely aware of the energies surrounding them. This sensitivity manifests both emotionally and physically, making them particularly receptive to the emotions of others and the dynamics of the environments they inhabit. They may respond intensely to the feelings of those around them or to external stimuli, which can sometimes be challenging for parents and educators to understand.

If your child reacts strongly to external stimuli or the emotions of others, they may be an Indigo, possessing a spiritual connection and awareness that often surpasses their years.

## 2. Extraordinary Intuition

Indigo children are often characterized by extraordinary intuition that goes far beyond what is typical for their age. Your child may demonstrate insights or knowledge that seem to stem from an inexplicable inner wisdom. These children often grasp complex concepts or have profound insights without any logical explanation or prior learning.

If your child shows sharp understanding or anticipates situations with surprising accuracy, it could be a sign of their Indigo nature. These intuitive abilities, though sometimes difficult to interpret, often reflect a deep connection to their spiritual essence and heightened sensitivity to surrounding energies.

## 3. Artistic Talents and Spiritual Sensitivity

Indigo children frequently show early artistic talents and spiritual sensitivity, revealing an extraordinary depth of soul for their age. They are often instinctively drawn to music, art, meditation, or other forms of spiritual expression, finding in these practices a way to channel and explore their rich inner world.

If your child demonstrates a marked and consistent interest in creative or spiritual activities, this could be a sign of their Indigo sensitivity—a reflection of their innate quest for meaning and their need to express themselves beyond conventional limits.

## 4. Nonconformity

Indigo children rarely settle for following pre-established paths; they prefer to carve their own way, guided by the unique light of their soul. Their pioneering spirit drives them to explore new perspectives, challenge conventions, and seek deeper truths.

Indigos often exhibit an instinctive aversion to authority they perceive as unjust or arbitrary. If your child tends to question or resist rules they find meaningless or unfair, it could be an expression of their Indigo spirit. This ability to challenge and reject blind obedience is not just a sign of their nonconformity but also an indication of their profound desire for justice and authenticity in the world around them.

### 5. Deep Connection with Nature

Indigo children have a natural and profound connection to nature that extends far beyond merely enjoying time outdoors. For them, animals are not just creatures but true friends and spiritual guides.

Whether it's petting a cat, feeding birds in a park, or walking through a forest searching for signs of wildlife, these interactions reinforce their sense of belonging to the living world. Their bond with nature is a fundamental part of their being, allowing them to feel connected to the essence of life itself.

### 6. Sense of Mission and Destiny

Indigo children often possess a strong sense of mission or destiny, which manifests from a young age through deep reflections on how they want to contribute to the world. Your child might share ideas about helping others, improving society, or making a positive impact.

These aspirations are not merely childhood dreams but genuine expressions of their unique potential and profound connection to a higher purpose.

### 7. Generational Disconnect

Indigo children may sometimes feel disconnected from their generation, displaying interests or perspectives more aligned with older individuals or a more mature worldview. This difference can make it difficult for them to integrate with peers, often leaving them feeling at odds with their age group.

If your child shows signs of this disconnection, it could indicate their Indigo nature, which drives them to seek deeper and more meaningful relationships and conversations.

Raising Indigo children, who are deeply sensitive and spiritually connected, requires a parenting approach that transcends conventional methods. These children, often described as possessing wisdom beyond their years and an intuitive understanding of the world, thrive in an environment filled with compassion, active listening, and freedom from toxic behaviors.

If you've found yourself asking:

*"How can I be a mindful parent and guide my Indigo child toward their full potential?"*

Drawing from the numerous stories shared by readers of my blog, here are the essential qualities for becoming a mindful parent to Indigo children:

### 1. Active Listening

Take time to understand the unique nature of your Indigo child. Be attentive to their emotional needs and nurture their innate curiosity, which is often key to their full development.

Indigo children have heightened sensitivity, perceiving the energies and emotions around them with an intensity that can sometimes be overwhelming. Recognizing this sensitivity as a strength and creating an environment where it is both accepted and valued is essential. Encourage emotional expression through dialogue, art, or other creative outlets to help them channel this sensitivity constructively.

Offering patient, caring support means being present to listen, not necessarily to solve their problems immediately. This builds trust and confidence in themselves and their perceptions. A child who feels supported is more likely to thrive and contribute positively to their environment.

### 2. Encouraging Creativity

Nurture their creativity by providing vibrant, stimulating environments. Introduce a variety of artistic activities, such as drawing, painting, music, or theater, allowing them to explore different forms of self-expression. Offer books that inspire and challenge their curiosity.

Create play areas that encourage experimentation and free invention. These spaces can include a small DIY workshop, an outdoor play area, or a cozy reading nook. Such opportunities help them develop unique talents and reinforce their confidence in expressing their vision of the world.

### 3. Open and Empathetic Communication

Foster open and honest communication with your child. Indigo children value transparency and seek genuine understanding. Encourage them to express their thoughts and feelings freely, ensuring they feel heard and respected.

Recognize and validate their emotions, even when they differ from your own, as this builds their sense of being understood. This creates a foundation of trust that encourages ongoing open dialogue, fostering their self-esteem and helping them navigate the world with confidence.

### 4. Holistic Education

Indigo children often show an early interest in spiritual or esoteric topics, reflecting their natural connection to concepts beyond the material world. Support this inclination by providing a holistic education that nurtures their curiosity and respects their desire to explore deeper aspects of existence.

Encourage artistic and spiritual exploration through activities such as meditation, mythology studies, or creative writing. Introduce age-appropriate meditative practices to help them cultivate inner peace and connect with their spiritual essence.

By fostering an environment that supports these interests, you nurture their intellectual, emotional, and spiritual growth, helping them thrive in a complex, interconnected world.

### 5. Balancing Rules and Freedom

Provide a harmonious balance of structure and freedom. Indigo children thrive in environments where clear guidelines offer stability while still allowing room for exploration and autonomy.

These children often exhibit a strong desire for independence and decision-making. Encourage this by offering age-appropriate responsibilities, opportunities to solve problems independently, and the freedom to organize their time. Allowing them to follow their intuition and take the initiative not only strengthens their self-reliance but also nurtures a sense of accomplishment and purpose.

## 6. Spiritual Practices

If your family practices spirituality, such as prayer or meditation, share these with your child in ways that are appropriate for their age and understanding. Indigo children often possess a deep, innate spiritual connection that guides them in their journey.

Family meditation moments can provide a space of calm and reflection, while discussions about spiritual themes help them explore their questions and develop a deeper understanding of the world. Spending time in nature is another powerful way to foster this connection, as Indigo children often find harmony and inspiration in natural surroundings.

Supporting your child's exploration of spirituality equips them with the tools to navigate the world with a sense of serenity and connection to something greater than themselves.

## 7. Parenting with Love and Wisdom

Raising an Indigo child requires an approach that blends love with wisdom. Each child is unique, endowed with specific talents, sensitivities, and challenges. Parenting, especially with an Indigo child, calls for constant adaptability and exceptional listening skills.

By fostering a warm, loving, and understanding environment, you allow your child's sensitive soul to flourish fully. This environment should be a sanctuary where the child feels safe to express their emotions and thoughts, and where their individuality is not only accepted but celebrated. Recognizing and valuing the deep emotional intelligence and strong intuition that often characterize Indigo children is crucial.

This involves nurturing their natural curiosity, supporting their passions, and providing the freedom to explore the world while also offering clear guidance. The balance between freedom and structure is key, allowing the child to feel both guided and independent.

As a parent, your role extends beyond protection to nourishing your child's soul. This can happen through deep conversations, moments of shared meditation, or simply being present and listening with kindness.

Ultimately, as the parent of an Indigo child, you play a pivotal role in their development and fulfillment. By offering unconditional love and profound understanding, you help them discover and realize their unique potential while equipping them with the tools to navigate a world that can often feel overwhelming to such sensitive and intuitive souls.

## 8. Eliminating Toxic Behaviors

Creating a home free of toxic behaviors is vital when raising Indigo children. These children are especially sensitive to negative energies, and prolonged exposure to toxic dynamics can significantly hinder their emotional and spiritual growth. As a parent, it's essential to model positive behavior, demonstrating kindness and fostering values of respect and compassion within the family.

Peaceful conflict resolution is equally critical. Indigo children deeply feel tensions and disagreements, which can impact them more than is outwardly apparent. Encouraging open communication, practicing active listening, and seeking harmonious solutions are crucial steps to maintaining a serene and secure family atmosphere.

Removing toxic dynamics within the family requires recognizing and addressing behaviors that might create a negative environment, whether intentional or not. This includes managing stress, controlling excessive emotional reactions, and adopting practices that support the emotional and mental balance of all family members.

Raising an Indigo child requires a mindful approach characterized by patience and benevolence. By providing an environment that not only avoids toxic influences but actively nurtures their special nature, you play a key role in their harmonious development. Creating a space where your child feels safe, valued, and understood helps them grow with confidence, enabling them to express their full potential and make positive contributions to the world around them.

Everything became clear in my mind, as if the pieces of a complex puzzle were finally coming together. The need to delve deeper into my research on Indigo adults was no longer just a curiosity but a true mission. I understood that exploring and sharing this knowledge with the world wouldn't merely be a transmission of the information I had gathered—it would be a crucial contribution to the collective awakening of humanity.

Indigo adults, with their heightened sensitivity, extraordinary intuition, and profound connection to the spiritual dimension, represent a valuable yet often misunderstood facet of human singularity. Their existence and unique experience on this Earth enrich our global understanding of the variety of human experiences. In many ways, they are messengers of change, bearers of light that illuminates unexplored paths.

As I continued to explore this topic, I realized that my goal wasn't just to uncover the mysteries surrounding these remarkable individuals, but also to provide guidance—a compass for those who, like them, feel different and are searching for their place in a world that often struggles to understand them. My work extended beyond mere observation; it involved diving deep into the recesses of human consciousness, discovering and elevating these precious souls who embody essential qualities for collective evolution.

This endeavor began to feel like a genuine life mission. It wasn't just a pursuit of knowledge or a personal passion—it was a necessary contribution to broadening our understanding of what it means to be human in all our diversity and complexity. Promoting awareness of Indigo people became a means of not only enlightening others about this reality but also fostering greater acceptance of diverse forms of intelligence, sensitivity, and perception of the world.

As I walked this path, I realized my role was to serve as a bridge between these sensitive souls and the rest of humanity, helping to weave bonds of understanding and mutual respect. This work, though challenging, is a way to contribute to the growth of our society by fully embracing diversity and recognizing the invaluable worth of each individual, whether they identify as Indigo or not.

Thus, my commitment to this cause endures, strengthened by the certainty that by illuminating the path for others, I am contributing to the creation of a more aware, empathetic, and, above all, human world.

## 10 THE MISSION OF THE INDIGOS ON EARTH

*"The meaning of life is to find your gift. The purpose of life is to share it."* — Pablo Picasso

*"Each of us has a unique vocation or mission in life... We must discover our own path, the one only we can follow."* — Viktor Frankl

*"We do not create our destinies; we come to understand them."* — Georges Bernanos

There is a space between sleep and wakefulness—a state where I'm not entirely sure if I'm dreaming or fully awake. In this liminal space, a window sometimes opens in the mind, allowing something to slip through. What I mean by 'something' is difficult to define; perhaps I might call it intuition, though in a broader, more expansive sense. I'm certain you know what I mean. It feels like an entire block of knowledge—thoughts, impressions, emotions, sensations, sounds, colors—flooding into my awareness all at once. It's an intense flow that overwhelms every fiber of my being, and I have no control over when it happens.

That morning, it happened again. I was either asleep, or perhaps not—I couldn't tell. A voice whispered a phrase, and every cell in my body vibrated with it, as if the entire universe resonated in harmony with this message:

## Are You an Indigo Adult?

*"My ambition is my destiny seeking to fulfill itself."*

New questions rose to the surface of my mind, questions that seemed to come from the depths of my consciousness, urging me to delve deeper into the meaning of my existence and the direction of my path:

*"What is my destiny? Is there a life mission I must understand to fully realize myself and maximize my innate potential?"*

For centuries, philosophers, mystics, and visionaries have pondered the purpose of human existence on Earth. Amid this search for meaning, a new generation of souls has emerged, often referred to as Indigos. Their presence on this planet is no coincidence; they have a profound spiritual mission to fulfill.

It is well known that Indigo adults are deeply sensitive beings, gifted with extraordinary intuition and a unique perspective on the world around them. Their energy is vibrant, their spirit free, and their hearts filled with compassion. They carry within them an inner light that shines with remarkable intensity, guiding them along the path of their spiritual mission.

*"But what is this mission?"*

To truly understand the mission of Indigo adults, we must delve into the depths of their essence. Their mission goes far beyond leading an ordinary life; it aims to bring profound transformation to the collective consciousness of humanity. Indigo adults aspire to make a positive impact, and their need to "do something" must find a meaningful outlet.

Let me share with you insights about the mission of Indigo adults, helping you uncover clues to discover your own life's mission:

❖ **Indigo Adults as Bearers of Knowledge**

> Indigo adults serve as beacons of wisdom, inviting others to embrace a broader reality, transcend the limitations of the mind, and connect with the spiritual dimension of existence. They are like lighthouses in the darkness, guiding others toward the light of truth and understanding. Through their unique perspective, they illuminate pathways to deeper awareness and inspire those around them to seek higher meaning.

### ❖ Indigo Adults as Healers of the Soul

With profound empathy and the ability to absorb the emotions of others, Indigo adults act as channels of healing for those in pain. Their presence soothes troubled hearts, offering comfort and solace to those in need. At the same time, they are deeply intolerant of injustice and stand firmly beside the vulnerable and marginalized. Their acute sensitivity drives them to champion the values of justice, equality, and compassion, actively opposing discrimination and oppression in all forms.

### ❖ Indigo Adults as Agents of Change

Their innovative spirit and courage to challenge the status quo make Indigo adults pioneers of transformation. They question entrenched social structures and norms, pushing humanity toward a new era of consciousness where love, compassion, and cooperation replace fear, division, and competition. They are visionaries who inspire progress and guide collective evolution through their unwavering commitment to positive change.

### ❖ Indigo Adults as Guardians of the Earth

Deeply connected to nature and respectful of all forms of life, Indigo adults are natural protectors of the planet. They advocate for environmental preservation, defend fragile ecosystems, and speak up for endangered species. Their bond with the natural world is instinctive and profound, as if they can feel the whispers of leaves in the wind and the heartbeat of the Earth itself.

Indigo adults often feel an essential need to spend time immersed in nature, finding renewal and regeneration in the serene beauty of trees, flowers, and plants. This connection is not merely restorative but deeply spiritual, grounding them in the rhythms of life.

Likewise, Indigo adults share a special affinity with animals, feeling profound empathy for their well-being and suffering. They are drawn to the companionship of animals and often form meaningful, enduring bonds with them. Whether caring for pets or advocating for animal rights, their connection to the animal kingdom reflects their deep respect for all living beings and their role as stewards of the Earth's intricate web of life.

In summary, the spiritual mission of Indigo adults is a quest for light, love, and enlightenment. They are ambassadors of a new consciousness, architects of a better world, and guides to a higher reality. Their presence on Earth is a precious gift, a blessing for all of humanity.

If Indigo adults were to explain their mission directly, they might say something like this:

> *« My mission is to live among others, actively participate in daily life, and simultaneously awaken a deeper consciousness in those I encounter, simply through my authentic presence.*
> *I don't need to convince anyone, nor do I need to stand out or impose anything.*
> *Everything is perfect as it is, and my role is to be fully myself, utilizing my abilities to their fullest potential.*
> *My task is to offer a different perspective, to embody values of truth and compassion. I seek to improve this world by integrating mindfulness and presence into the most ordinary activities, helping others—both directly and indirectly—to remember their potential and to perceive the hidden beauty and depth in everyday life. »*

In this grand adventure that is life on Earth, each of us has a role to play. We are the actors of our existence, carefully choosing our place in this vast theater of humanity. But beyond our individual role lies a deeper design that guides our steps. When we discover this design, an inner light illuminates our path, transforming each day into an unparalleled adventure.

Life, of course, is not always simple, but it is in the moment we fully realize our purpose that our existence gains its true meaning.

## *"But how do we discover this purpose?"*

This is an essential question we all must answer. We discover it by listening to the whispers of our hearts, opening our minds to the possibility that our true purpose has always been within us, from the very beginning.

I do not claim that your search must necessarily have a spiritual connotation. However, it is vital that the fulfillment of this purpose brings you profound satisfaction. You must feel that you are doing exactly what you are here to do, without anyone imposing it upon you.

Here's a crucial point: your purpose is chosen by you, by your soul.

It is unique and does not conform to what society tries to impose on everyone uniformly. A compelling reflection supporting this idea is that, when we see someone fulfilling their purpose, we don't necessarily desire to do what they're doing—we are instead inspired to pursue our own.

Yet, if you still don't know your purpose, you must keep searching. Be curious, pursue this quest relentlessly until you discover it, because it is at that moment that life begins to hold its full meaning, and this search becomes our spiritual nourishment.

I see so many people wandering without knowing why they are here, failing even to search. For them, time serves only to grow older, to wait for something to happen... in vain. There is always something to do or experience to move closer to your purpose, and it is this pursuit that gives life its flavor.

Living without knowing our life's mission deprives the world of our best energies. To unlock our full potential and live a complete life, we must follow the path of our life's mission.

If you are a parent, the topic of life's mission takes on a special significance in relation to Indigo children. Indigo children have remarkably clear ideas and often act as our teachers. Paradoxically, we find ourselves teaching these young beings how to navigate this world, while they seem to possess an innate wisdom that far surpasses our understanding of things.

Indigo children, with their pure perception and deep connection to the essential, remind us that true knowledge does not always lie in the experiences we've accumulated, but in the simplicity and clarity of their outlook on life.

If Indigo children were to articulate their mission directly, they might say something like this:

> *"We are here to bring love, compassion, and light into this world.*
> *Our mission is to awaken sleeping hearts, heal the wounds of the Earth, and restore harmony among all living beings, simply through our gentleness.*
> *In the depth of our gaze lies the understanding that we are guardians of truth and wisdom. Our presence on this planet is an invitation to spiritual awakening and collective transformation.*
> *We are the artisans of change, the catalysts of consciousness, and the bearers of light in the shadows of ignorance. It is within our questions that our teachings reside.*
> *We are here on Earth to help build the awareness and structures for a new world—a world that will be more harmonious, more beautiful, more just, and more peaceful.*
> *We all long for this peace, we all seek happiness, and one day, we will all attain it. This is our shared purpose."*

As for me, I feel a deep desire to inspire those around me by exploring the hidden realms of self-knowledge and unveiling essential truths uncovered through my personal journey. I do this primarily through writing books that offer pathways for growth to those seeking profound answers and a possible route toward their own fulfillment.

Through my writing, I aim to convey powerful cosmologies that enrich the mind and nourish the soul, allowing the seeds of human potential to fully bloom and the inner light to shine with renewed brilliance. My intention is to act as a catalyst for personal and collective development, providing guidance that helps each individual reconnect with their divine essence and life's mission.

By writing, I aspire to reveal the hidden beauty in everyday life, to connect readers to the primordial energies of nature, and to embody values of truth and compassion. In doing so, I contribute to building a new world—more harmonious, just, and peaceful—honoring the mysteries of life and the ancestral wisdom that calls us to transform our reality.

One final thought on this subject: Indigo individuals manifest their mission in diverse ways, each essential for the emergence of a new paradigm.

Some dedicate themselves to action, channeling their energy into designing and implementing new models of living that address the needs of a transforming world. They focus on creating innovative housing systems, redefining food supply chains, reimagining education, and developing groundbreaking approaches to health. Their work goes beyond improving existing systems; it aims to establish entirely new frameworks rooted in values of respect, cooperation, and harmony with nature and humanity.

Others choose the role of observant and enlightened witnesses. Their mission is to absorb, analyze, and integrate the profound changes occurring around them, thereby accumulating valuable wisdom. These individuals serve as silent witnesses to the world's transformations, striving to deeply understand the dynamics at play so that, at the right moment, they can share these insights and apply them thoughtfully. Though less visible, their work is equally crucial, laying the groundwork for future progress and supporting the collective evolution of consciousness.

Finally, there are those whose mission is even more introspective. These Indigo souls are here to experience their spiritual ascension, walking a path akin to that of sages and saints throughout the ages. Their presence on Earth is itself a source of inspiration; they embody the possibility of profound inner transformation and become living examples of what it means to live in harmony with the divine. Their contemplative journey serves as a constant reminder that spiritual evolution is an ongoing process and that each of us has the potential to reach higher levels of consciousness.

Each role—whether active, observant, or introspective—holds immense value in the grand tapestry of humanity's spiritual evolution.

Ask yourself these questions:

*What are my most important goals?*
*What relationships will I build to help me achieve my purpose?*

I'd like to conclude with the words of Brazilian author Paulo Coelho, who in 1997 published Manual of the Warrior of Light, where he writes:

> *"Warriors of the light are recognizable at first glance. They are in the world, and they are part of it. Often, they find their lives to lack meaning. Yet, they have not given up on seeking it. They question, they reflect. They reject passivity and fatalism. This is why they are warriors of the light."*

## 11 HOW TO BREAK FREE FROM OUR PRISON

**Frodo:** "I wish the Ring had never come to me. I wish none of this had happened."

**Gandalf:** "So do all who live to see such times. But that is not for them to decide. All we have to decide is what to do with the time that is given to us."

*"Are we living in the Matrix, as depicted in the movie The Matrix?"*

In that film, a sophisticated software creates a virtual reality that enslaves humanity, ensuring that people live unaware of their true condition, controlled by a machine. If you take a closer look at your daily reality, you might come to an unsettling conclusion: everything seems to resemble that film more than you might have imagined.

*"How do we escape it?"*

Life, as we know it, is a cycle of repetition. You wake up, go to work, come home to eat dinner, and then start the cycle all over again. This relentless rhythm leaves little room to understand what truly matters to you, to care for yourself, or to spend meaningful time with the people who remind you of who you really are. It's as if an unceasing flow of thoughts keeps you imprisoned, making you live on autopilot, trapped in a Matrix just like the one in the movie.

*"Darling, you seem so absorbed by all this lately,"* my girlfriend said one evening as we sat at the table.

*"Is something bothering you?"*

I paused, searching for the words to explain what I was feeling.

*"It's hard to put into words,"* I said. *"But I feel compelled to share what I'm discovering about indigo people and spirituality. It's like..."*

I trailed off, trying to organize my thoughts. What I felt was profound, a call to explore and share knowledge that seemed to rise from the depths of my soul. It wasn't just intellectual curiosity but an authentic desire to help others see the world with fresh eyes, to rediscover their true selves, and to break free from the Matrix that keeps us trapped.

*"It's a vital part of my personal growth,"* I continued, *"and I want to help others connect with their own truth."*

She smiled warmly, understanding my need to share this discovery with the world.

*"I support you wholeheartedly,"* she said. *"If it's something you're passionate about, follow that path. I'm sure you'll touch people's hearts with what you have to share."*

Her encouragement was exactly what I needed. With her support, I decided to embark on this journey and create a blog where I could share my reflections, discoveries, and experiences about indigo people and spirituality. In a short time, the blog's success exceeded my wildest expectations. It quickly attracted millions of readers worldwide, eager to share their own experiences and connect with others who shared similar ideas. It was incredible to see how hungry people were for knowledge and understanding on this topic.

That blog no longer exists in its original form. As I mentioned, it has transformed into this book, and I hope it can reach even more people who might not have otherwise encountered this information. It became my way of escaping the Matrix, albeit temporarily.

The Matrix compels you to constantly chase deadlines, meet objectives, and complete tasks. You're so busy juggling commitments that there's no time left—especially for yourself. This relentless pace can desensitize you, pulling you away from the deeper, more meaningful aspects of life and leaving you with a sense of incompleteness.

*"So, how do we reconnect with what truly matters?"*
The first step is to become aware of this mechanism.

Recognize that you might be trapped in a routine dictated not by your genuine desires but by the expectations of others. It's essential to give yourself permission to slow down, reflect, and ask yourself the right questions:

*What truly matters to me?*

*What makes me come alive, giving my life profound meaning?*

Once you identify what's essential, reorganize your daily life to make room for those things. This might mean saying no to certain commitments, adjusting your priorities, and carving out time for yourself each day—even if it's just a few minutes.

Meditate, spend time in nature, engage in activities that excite you, and surround yourself with people who inspire and support you.

Reconnecting with what matters most won't happen overnight, but every step in this direction will help you break free from the suffocating Matrix and move toward a more authentic life aligned with your true self.

Our reality is a Matrix of perceptions shaped by our minds, culture, and self-imposed limitations. Indigo adults don't easily conform to existing belief systems. They resist the deceptive promises of an oligarchic system centered on self-interest and devoid of scruples. Indigo individuals deeply feel the lack of freedom and clash with the repressive dogmas imposed by society and religious institutions. They understand that those who make the rules and laws often wield no more legitimacy than anyone else. They see that this power is frequently usurped and used to serve personal interests, maintaining an unjust position of dominance.

These souls are here to transform social structures rooted in democratic illusions, oppressive traditions, and control mechanisms imposed by a minority at the expense of collective well-being. Indigo individuals expose ideological conflicts and power struggles that fuel fear, hatred, and distrust among people.

They strive to dismantle unjust systems that disregard the most vulnerable and destroy, through violence and exploitation, the Earth's natural resources—resources that belong to all humanity. Indigo adults are often described as having a specific life mission: to catalyze change and restore balance in our relationships with the environment, society, and one another. Their revolutionary vision rejects established rules and the status quo. Their acute sensitivity and sincere desire to promote others' well-being drive them to take action and create a new balance in the world.

Indigo adults do not settle for going with the flow or conforming to existing norms. They question social structures and entrenched systems that perpetuate injustice, discord, and emotional suffering. Their desire for change propels them to take bold and innovative actions, often outside conventional frameworks, to advance their vision of a better world.

Indigos are revolutionaries at heart, ready to overcome obstacles and break down barriers to fulfill their mission. Their unique perspective and ability to see beyond appearances enable them to understand society's deepest needs and propose creative solutions that inspire others.

Their journey is not without challenges, as their sensitivity makes them vulnerable to negative energies and social pressures. However, this very sensitivity fuels their compassion and empathy, driving them to persist in their quest for transformation.

In conclusion, indigos embody the hope for positive change. Their commitment to restoring harmony in our world and promoting understanding and unity among people is a powerful force essential for evolving society toward a more balanced and sustainable future.

If you've realized that you are an indigo and have decided to escape your Matrix, know that there's no universal formula for everyone.

However, there are proven strategies for change that I can share with you.

### Strategy 1: Reprogram Your Subconscious

*"Until you make the unconscious conscious, it will direct your life, and you will call it fate."* — C. Jung.

Your subconscious is like an archive that stores all the information you've gathered since birth, constantly feeding bits of it to your conscious mind. Imagine your subconscious as a field where you plant seeds to harvest later. If you neglect this field and let it run wild, others may plant their own seeds of fear and expectations, shaping it to serve the Matrix.

The subconscious can be reprogrammed using the power of intention and emotions. Even without your full awareness, your subconscious shapes your reality. The good news is that you can change these patterns to make them more positive and free yourself from the Matrix's grip. While your thoughts play a key role in this process, they aren't enough on their own. You primarily communicate with your subconscious through emotions.

It's essential to align the power of your thoughts with your emotions. By becoming aware of your fears, accepting them, and fostering positive intentions aligned with your true desires, your ability to manifest your dreams grows exponentially.

## Strategy 2: View Challenges as Opportunities

Your thoughts influence your reality. By changing how you perceive your experiences, you can quickly transform your emotions as well. If you feel trapped by the Matrix, that frustration can become the catalyst to move toward your dreams and clarify what truly matters to you.

It's not easy to wake up early, commute, and spend the best hours of your day at a job that might not excite you, just to pay bills and buy groceries. But this shouldn't be an excuse to ignore your heart and your deepest desires. We stop pursuing our dreams when we listen to voices that limit us with their ideas of how life "should" be.

Many of us may not yet know our true passions or interests because we've been taught not to value anything outside the home-work-bed routine. But there's nothing more important than what you genuinely love. Start connecting with this deeper dimension of yourself.

View your current situation as a challenge that helps you grow and understand yourself better by contrasting what you're living with what you truly wish to experience. You are far more powerful than you've been led to believe. Take back your power.

### Strategy 3: Make Time Meaningful

You may often feel rushed to meet deadlines, fulfill expectations, or avoid disappointing others. Perhaps you're afraid you won't be good enough or capable enough. If so, take a moment for yourself and recognize that everything is in constant motion. Nothing in life is certain except that one day we will leave this world.

Sleep, rest, immerse yourself in nature, and spend time with loved ones. Do things that feel meaningful in the present moment, not just because you planned them in the past or hope to achieve something in the future. Pursue what you love, knowing that everything is subject to change. Ultimately, what will matter most is having appreciated your journey.

### Strategy 4: Notice the Signs Around You

When life becomes a routine, you naturally desensitize yourself and stop noticing signs or synchronicities—those small coincidences that can help you create balance in your life and increase awareness.

Have you ever noticed how magical traveling to a foreign place feels? Visiting a new destination can reset your mind and help your eyes rediscover sensitivity. Take time to explore places you've never been before.

### Strategy 5: Take Care of Your Diet

When stressed, you may resort to foods that intoxicate your body and desensitize you even further. Introduce more fruits and vegetables into your diet and drink plenty of water. Try this for a while and observe how it affects your mind and health.

What you eat and drink carries information. The Matrix loses its grip on you when you change the information you introduce into your body.

### Strategy 6: Learn to Say No

Learn to say no—to your friends, family, or even your boss (when possible). When we can't say no, we become emotional sponges, overly sensitive to the needs of those around us while neglecting our own. This can leave you feeling overwhelmed and silenced

This is a crucial moment for you, a time for introspection and self-discovery. If you wish to move forward on this path, you must be ready to assert yourself, which includes saying no when necessary.

As you continue this journey, you will meet new, positive people who reflect your evolving path. Embrace these connections to share progress and continue growing together.

### Strategy 7: Spend Time in Nature

Whether alone or with others, take time to breathe deeply in a green space. Focus on your breath as you observe the trees. Relax. Oxygenate yourself. Engage in physical activity. Allow yourself to live fully in your body. Nature is a reservoir of positive vibrations that helps you reconnect with your true essence and frees you from the Matrix's influence.

### Strategy 8: Cultivate Your Passions

You may have put your passions aside for years, but deep down, you know who you want to be and what you want to do. Your passions lead you to become the best version of yourself, attracting more success, love, and well-being. You might think pursuing your true desires is unimportant, but the opposite is true: it's your path out of the Matrix.

### Strategy 9: Step Outside Your Comfort Zone

Action is essential. Step outside your comfort zone. Try new things, meet new people, and explore unfamiliar places. Act to advance your projects and plans. Write down all your new ideas and take the first step immediately—don't delay.

### Strategy 10: Cultivate Deep Gratitude

Recognize all the beautiful things in your life today and be grateful for them. Visualize the change you want in your life and express gratitude as if it has already happened. Gratitude has the power to "disconnect" you from the Matrix. By doing this, you'll build a new reality guided by your desires and emotions.

**Strategy 11: Explore Your Mind**

This inner journey has the power to reveal your truth and help you escape the illusions of the Matrix. When you discover your truth, you begin to create your reality consciously. You pierce the veil of illusion, letting go of what doesn't serve you—everything unimportant that complicates your life. By clearing your mind, you can focus on what truly matters. At this point, you start vibrating at the frequency of love instead of fear. The Matrix gradually loses its grip on you.

This doesn't mean isolating yourself from society but rather living consciously and freely within it.

Breaking free from your personal Matrix isn't just about escaping an oppressive routine; it's about opening the path to a more authentic life, one that aligns with your deepest values. Take a moment to reflect:
*"What are the chains holding you captive? What does true freedom mean to you?"*
I began writing because it resonates with my essence and allows me to express myself fully.
Ask yourself this:
*"What aligns my being with my truth?"*
In other words:
*"What steps can you take today to move closer to that genuine freedom, the kind that connects you to who you truly are?"*

# 12 INDIGO ADULTS AND THE POLITICS OF OUR TIME

*"The future belongs to those who believe in the beauty of their dreams."* — Eleanor Roosevelt

*"We must be the change we wish to see in the world."* — Mahatma Gandhi

*"The only way to predict the future is to create it."* — Peter Drucker

Indigo adults reject conventional belief systems and resist the promises of current power structures. They clearly perceive the lack of freedom and the repressive dogmas imposed by society and religion. They understand that those who establish rules and laws wield no greater power or legitimacy than anyone else. Indigo adults are here to transform a society built on illusions of democracy, restrictive traditions, and control mechanisms imposed by a minority at the expense of the common good. They denounce ideological divisions and power struggles that fuel fear, hatred, and mistrust among people. Many recognize that they live within a system of control, shaped by lies and illusions, where the primary interests revolve around profit and maintaining the dominance of a select elite.

The indomitable drive for growth and expansion among Indigo adults is not rooted in competition but in a profound desire for communion with others and the universe around them. This drive stems from a heightened spiritual awareness and an amplified sensitivity to the subtle energies of the world.

As an Indigo adult, you feel an intrinsic connection to the very essence of life, compelling you to seek fulfillment that transcends the material and tangible. Your quest for growth is fueled by an insatiable thirst for knowledge, understanding, and self-realization. You constantly strive to explore new dimensions of existence, develop your intuitive and creative abilities, and draw ever closer to your true essence.

You envision a model of personal and collective development that surpasses traditional economic paradigms. You imagine an economy where cooperation replaces competition and resources are distributed equitably, honoring the unique talents of every individual. For you, growth is not merely the accumulation of material wealth but a holistic process of evolving the spirit, body, and soul.

In this innovative economic model, respect for the environment takes center stage. The peaceful and symbiotic coexistence between humans, animals, nature, and the planet would no longer be a utopia but a tangible reality. Social and economic structures would be reimagined to promote sustainability, kindness, and interconnectedness. Every living being could thrive in balance and harmony, fostering a society where progress is no longer measured by material wealth but by the quality of human relationships and the overall health of our planetary ecosystem. With your clear vision and determination, you position yourself as a catalyst for this transformation, guiding humanity toward a future where progress is achieved not at the expense of the Earth but in perfect symbiosis with it.

Your ambition for expansion is not selfish; it is deeply rooted in the desire to see all beings live in balance, to witness an economy that serves humanity rather than the reverse, and to watch the planet flourish. This perspective challenges traditional values, placing connection, collaboration, and mutual respect at the forefront. It proposes a model where every action is infused with awareness, and every decision is made with its global impact in mind.

Ultimately, Indigo adults like you carry within themselves the seeds of a peaceful yet profound revolution, capable of shaping a world where harmony between humanity and nature is finally restored. Too often, societal expectations and pressures from those around us shape our own expectations for the future, leading to repeated disappointments because they fail to reflect our true desires. To change your destiny, it is essential to identify your authentic aspirations.

It takes optimism and courage to overcome conditioning, to reclaim responsibility for your destiny, and, most importantly, to live with a profound joy that serves as your guide in every circumstance. Regardless of past experiences that may have eroded your confidence in the future, this inner joy must become your beacon.

As an Indigo adult, your unique sensitivity and advanced consciousness drive you to seek a life rich in meaning and authenticity. Yet, in a world often governed by societal expectations and external power structures, it can be challenging to fully connect with your desires and deepest aspirations. This is precisely why the following exercise, inspired by the methods of Igor Sibaldi, will be particularly beneficial for you[5].

This exercise is designed to help you reconnect with your deepest aspirations and break free from the limitations that hinder your growth. By taking the time to reflect and write down what you truly desire, you begin to build a clear vision of what truly matters to you and what can genuinely enrich your life.

Indigo adults like you often feel a natural drive for expansion and authentic connection. By identifying and pursuing your desires, you can open doors to new possibilities and transform your reality. This exercise is not just a tool for personal development but a way to reclaim your inner power and align your life with your values and passions.

**How to Proceed:**

- ❖ Prepare Two Notebooks: Find a quiet place where you can focus without distractions.

---

[5] Igor Sibaldi is a renowned author, lecturer, and researcher in the fields of spirituality and personal development. Sibaldi is also a recognized translator and scholar, particularly celebrated for his in-depth studies on Dostoevsky and Russian culture. Through his translations and literary works, he has conveyed the profound essence of the Russian soul, delving into the great philosophical and existential questions that permeate Dostoevsky's writings.

Sibaldi's innovative approach is widely admired for its exploration of the deeper dimensions of the human psyche and its emphasis on the transformative potential of self-awareness. His work encourages individuals to uncover their authentic desires and take conscious steps toward creating a more fulfilling and meaningful life.

❖ Write 200 Desires: In the first notebook, list 200 precise and achievable desires. Start with small, simple wishes and gradually move to bigger, more ambitious dreams.

❖ Use the phrase "I want…" for each desire.

❖ Select 101 Desires: Once you've written your 200 desires, choose the 101 that feel most important to you right now and copy them into the second notebook.

**Examples:**

❖ I want to learn how to cook exotic dishes.
❖ I want to go hiking in the mountains.
❖ I want to take a photography course.

**Guidelines:**

❖ Use "I want…" to begin each desire.
❖ Avoid using negations like "not" or "don't."
❖ Focus on achievable desires.
❖ Think about the goal, not the means to achieve it.
❖ Avoid making wishes for others or comparing yourself to others.
❖ Each desire must be unique and specific.
❖ Keep each desire concise, using no more than 14 words.
❖ Don't include desires that impose expectations on others, whether in romantic or other relationships.

As you work through this exercise, you may find it surprisingly difficult to list 200 genuine desires. This is normal and reveals how often we overlook or suppress our true aspirations. Remember, this is not about making wishes to a genie; it's about facing yourself and your blank page. *"Are you sure of what you truly want?"*

Why 200 Desires? The goal is to go beyond superficial wishes and dive into the depths of your true aspirations. Writing 200 desires forces you to explore every facet of your dreams, uncovering parts of yourself that you may have overlooked or ignored.

Why 101 Desires? The number 101 represents ongoing growth. The extra one beyond 100 symbolizes that this work is never static—it continually evolves and challenges you to think beyond your limits.

### Daily Practice:

Once you've copied your 101 desires into the second notebook, read them every day for 365 days. Over time, you'll notice that some of these desires begin to manifest. When they do, cross them off and replace them with new ones, perhaps from your original list.

### Reflect and Evolve:

Ask yourself:
*Which desires are coming true?*
*Which are not? Why?*
This reflection will provide invaluable insights into your motivations, priorities, and the obstacles you may face.

After one year, destroy both notebooks by burning them and let go of the process. By then, you will have gained clarity about what you truly desire and learned how to focus on what genuinely matters for your future. This exercise is not just a list—it's a transformative journey that pushes you to face your fears, overcome insecurities, and align with your authentic self.

For an Indigo adult, this exercise provides a profound opportunity to reconnect with your true essence, unlock your potential, and live a life filled with meaning and joy. Dedicate this time to yourself, give value to your desires, and let them guide you toward a brighter, more authentic future.

# 13 THE DARK NIGHT OF THE SOUL: WHAT TO DO WHEN EVERYTHING GOES WRONG?

*"To reach where you are not, you must pass through where you are not. To come to possess everything, desire to possess nothing. To become everything, desire to be nothing."* — St. John of the Cross

*"The sole reason for man's existence is to delve deeply into himself, to ascend to the summit of his heart, and to keep walking without pause."* — Rainer Maria Rilke

*"Whoever looks outside dreams; whoever looks inside awakens."* — Carl Jung

I was still in that house, lost in the middle of the English countryside, one of those places where the silence feels so heavy it becomes almost oppressive. My partner had left, the one who had helped me create my first blog. Suddenly, I found myself alone, with a dog, a cat, and those empty rooms where the ticking of the clock echoed like the sound of solitude.

I tried to keep the business we had built together afloat, but I couldn't do it on my own. At the same time, a demanding job was consuming me entirely, draining every ounce of energy, while the world outside seemed to be falling apart.

The Dark Night of the Soul is a moment when everything you knew, everything you relied on, crumbles. It's a brutal but transformative invitation to look within, to face your fears, to strip away all that you are not, and to rediscover the most authentic core of your being.

**Learner:** Master, I feel lost. I don't know what to do. Everything around me is changing, even the people I trusted most. Every relationship, everything I've built, seems to be crumbling all at once.

**Master:** This is a sign that you're drawing closer to your deeper essence. This process may feel disorienting, but remember, it's part of your journey.

**Learner:** But I don't know which direction to take. I have so many questions, and I can't find answers. How can I know if I'm heading the right way?

**Master:** The right direction isn't something you find by looking outward. It's something you discover by listening within. When the outer world falls apart, it's an invitation to turn inward, to recognize what is truly yours and let go of what isn't. Take one step at a time, with trust. Don't seek immediate answers—the journey itself is the answer.

The **Master** paused to let the disciple reflect on his words, then continued:

It's essential to maintain trust in yourself, even when everything seems to be falling apart or when answers seem elusive. Moments of doubt and uncertainty are not failures; on the contrary, they often mean you're on the right path. Confusion and discomfort can be invitations to listen more closely to your intuition and trust the unique path that is yours alone.

**Learner:** Even if I understand what you're teaching me, I still feel lost. What can I do? What's the point of all this? Why do things never go the way I imagined?

**Master:** It's in these moments of profound questioning that you have the opportunity to reconnect with your true nature. Don't fear this uncertainty—immerse yourself in it. Often, through vulnerability, you'll uncover hidden aspects of yourself and feel more in tune with your real path. Remember, the journey is rarely linear, but it is always authentic.

**Learner:** In all this confusion, how can I stop feeling stuck?

**Master:** Trust the process and remember that every step, every choice—even every detour—is guiding you toward realizing your true self.

**Learner:** The questions that torment me are about discovering myself: who I really am and who I have yet to become. I feel as though a part of me wants to emerge, an inner voice pushing me to explore new horizons and break through old barriers. I feel so different, as though something greater is trying to manifest through me.

**Master:** It's not easy to confront these questions, as they often push us out of our comfort zones and into uncharted territories of the soul. But it's in these uncertainties and doubts that you'll find the key to your true essence. The journey to discovering yourself requires courage, but it's the only way to live in harmony with the person you are meant to become.

**Learner:** I've thought about this a lot, but I truly don't know what my passions are. I have so many interests. How can I know if I'm making the right choice? And even if I could change everything, how would I pay my mortgage? How can I be sure I can support my family while doing what I love?

**Master:** These questions are natural and common during times of transition and self-discovery. When we talk about the "path," I notice that people's greatest difficulty lies in not knowing which direction to take, fearing they'll make the wrong choice. This indecision can be paralyzing, creating discomfort and uncertainty that's hard to overcome.

**Learner:** You know me well—we always talk together. Can you help me figure out the right path for me?

**Master:** The question you're asking is deceptive because it's not the question you should be asking.

**Learner:** Why not? – becoming increasingly impatient.

**Master:** Because that question assumes there's a single, correct path for each of us. But that's not the case. Life isn't a series of binary choices where one is right, and the other is wrong. It's not a quiz. There isn't one predestined road you must find to succeed or be happy.

Moreover, asking, *"What's the right path?"* creates immense pressure. It implies that if we don't make the "right" choice, we'll have to live with the consequences of that mistake forever. This mindset can paralyze us, leaving us stuck in inertia.

Instead, I invite you to ask yourself, *"Which path brings me joy and allows me to fully express who I am today?"*

This question opens up possibilities and freedom. It acknowledges that there may be many right paths for you, as long as they resonate with your essence, your values, and your life's mission.

**Learner:** You're enlightening me, but I feel even more confused!

**Master:** Feeling confused or lost in the face of so many possibilities is entirely normal. The important thing is not to get trapped by the fear of making the wrong choice. Let yourself be guided by what makes you feel alive, even if it means taking risks or stepping out of your comfort zone. Remember, uncertainty is part of the journey. Often, the times when we feel most lost are when we're growing the most. Personal growth isn't linear; it's filled with detours, unexpected experiences, and hidden opportunities in moments of doubt or confusion.

**Learner:** So, what do you recommend I do to overcome this feeling of uncertainty?

**Master:** Stay curious and open. Trust your intuition and follow the signs that appear, even if they aren't immediately clear.

Sometimes, just having the courage to take the first step is enough for the path to reveal itself.

Ultimately, there is no "right" or "wrong" path. There's only your path—the one you choose to walk with courage, passion, and trust. That, in itself, is proof you're on the right track.

Instead, ask yourself, *"What's the next thing I want to try or do?"* Notice how this simple shift in perspective frees you. It removes an enormous emotional burden and significantly reduces stress.

You don't have to commit to one lifelong path. You can choose to try something for a month, six months, a year—it doesn't matter. What's important is understanding that it doesn't need to be the "right" path forever, just the next step in your process of discovery and growth.

The idea is to try new things, explore, and learn from every experience.

**Learner:** Perhaps you're right, but I feel so far from the life of my dreams, and I don't even know how to achieve it. Everything seems out of reach!

**Master:** We all have preconceived notions of what the "perfect life" should look like—the life of our dreams. For example, in my case, if I were a famous writer, I'd spend my days peacefully writing, sipping lemonade on the terrace of my garden overlooking the sea. But it's precisely this rigid vision that "blocks" us.

We constantly compare our current reality to this idealized life, and it makes us feel like something is wrong—that we've somehow failed or need to change everything radically. It's crucial to understand that these rigid and unrealistic expectations are what cause our frustration.

**Learner:** Now you've taken away all my certainties! The only thing I know for sure is that I know nothing!

**Master:** Perfect! That's an excellent starting point! Use this moment to create space within yourself, to quiet the mental noise, and reconnect with what your heart truly tells you. This moment of uncertainty also indicates that you're finally taking full responsibility for your life.

You're beginning to live in harmony with your essence and to honor your most authentic needs and desires. In other words, stop listening to all those voices in your head telling you what you "should" do, and listen more to your heart—the one guiding you toward your true path.

That's how you'll find the right road: your road.

As Antonio Machado said:

**"There is no path; the path is made by walking."**

Perhaps, like the Disciple in the dialogue, you too are going through a period of profound questioning, marked by frustration and a sense of being lost. These moments of "transition" are, in fact, valuable opportunities to reconnect with yourself, learn new things, shed limiting beliefs, and listen to your inner voice—the one that knows your true path.

There are certain signs, seemingly negative, that may actually indicate a deep realignment with your essence:

### 1. You Feel Lost

This sense of disorientation is actually a sign that you are becoming more grounded in the present moment and less preoccupied with how things "should" be. Instead of chasing an idealized and rigid image, you are learning to let go of expectations and external pressures. A new possibility emerges: building your reality based on what exists here and now. The idea of who you "should" be or what you "should" do starts to dissolve, freeing you from the weight of societal, familial, and self-imposed expectations.

It's a transition where, even if you feel lost, you are actually finding yourself. You allow yourself to explore without fear of not fitting a predefined image, embracing the uncertainty and beauty of being exactly where you are. This process of reconnection with the present is a sign that you are learning to trust the flow of life, allowing yourself to be who you truly are without judgment or the need to be different from your authentic self.

You begin to understand that you don't need to conform to what others expect of you and that your true strength lies in accepting your unique path. It's a fundamental step toward your inner freedom and genuine well-being.

## 2. You Feel Confused

Confusion can signal that you are stepping out of your comfort zone and beginning to question long-held certainties. This state of uncertainty may generate anxiety and unease, but it also indicates that you are reevaluating your true desires and deepest motivations. You are exploring new ways of being and thinking, prompting you to reassess what you once considered immutable.

This moment of confusion represents a critical phase for creating a life that aligns with your essence. It's like dismantling a puzzle to reassemble it in a way that better reflects who you are today, rather than the image of who you thought you needed to become. Confusion urges you to explore, question old habits and beliefs, and discover what truly resonates with your authentic self.

Instead of fearing this uncertainty, see it as an opportunity to reassess what you truly desire. Confusion can precede clarity—a transitional phase where you release expectations and external pressures, allowing yourself to identify what you genuinely want. It's a sign that you're taking control of your path, listening to your inner voice, and exploring new directions that align with your true nature.

## 3. You Struggle to Make Decisions

A temporary difficulty in decision-making may indicate that you are exploring new possibilities and are reluctant to limit yourself to a single predefined path. Rather than acting impulsively, you give yourself the time and space needed to consider different options, broadening your horizons. This might make you feel stuck or indecisive, but it's important to understand that this isn't a weakness; it's a phase of deep reflection.

You are carefully evaluating which direction to take, striving to avoid rushed decisions that might not reflect who you truly are or what you desire. This period of hesitation can be viewed as an opportunity to listen more attentively to your intuition and reflect on which paths could bring you closer to your true goals and essence.

It's not a sign of failure or lack of determination but a moment when you allow yourself to experiment and remain open to what may come. This phase requires time and contemplation, but through this process, you'll find the path that truly resonates with you.

## 4. You Feel Exhausted

This exhaustion may indicate that you are shedding stagnant energy or old beliefs that no longer serve you. It's a process of energetic cleansing, which can be tiring but is necessary to make room for the new. While this fatigue may feel uncomfortable, it's a sign that you are releasing what is no longer in harmony with you, allowing fresh, renewed energy to flow into your life.

Think of this moment as a sort of "inner cleaning": you are eliminating what weighs you down and slows your growth, making way for a more authentic existence. This process requires patience and kindness toward yourself but is an essential step in welcoming new possibilities, perspectives, and positive energies. This feeling of exhaustion isn't a signal to stop but an invitation to slow down, care for yourself, and respect your pace. It's a period of transition during which your body and mind are working to realign with what's best for you. Embrace this fatigue as part of the journey, knowing that through this process of energetic cleansing, you can emerge with renewed vitality and clarity.

## 5. Fear Holds You Back

The resistance you feel is a sign that you are on the verge of a significant breakthrough in your personal development. Often, this fear represents the last obstacle before a meaningful change. It's as though part of you is clinging to what is familiar, even if it no longer serves you.

This resistance manifests as fear, doubt, or procrastination—it's the weight holding you back. However, it also signals that you are nearing greater self-awareness and personal growth. Resistance doesn't mean you should stop; rather, it indicates that you are close to breaking old patterns and moving toward a new phase in your life.

Welcome this resistance as part of your journey. It's a sign that something important is about to emerge—that you are ready to let go of what limits you and embrace the new. Instead of avoiding or fearing it, approach it with curiosity and ask yourself what it's truly trying to tell you. Often, behind this resistance lies the key to a transformation that will bring you closer to your true essence and deepest goals.

Going through the Dark Night of the Soul means answering the call to reconnect with what truly matters. Every sign, every challenging phase is an open door to a life more aligned and authentic. Embrace these moments as allies on your journey, and remember: light is always born from darkness.

*"The path does not exist beforehand;
it is forged with every step you dare to take."*

## 14 HOW TO STOP ABSORBING OTHER PEOPLE'S EMOTIONS

*"Look deep within yourself; there is a source of power that will always flow if you continue to seek it."* — Marcus Aurelius Antoninus

*"You can never reach dawn without traveling through the path of night."* — Khalil Gibran

*"Emotions are the slaves of thoughts, and you are the slave of emotions."* — Elizabeth Gilbert

    In the labyrinths of fate, my eyes become lost in the enchanting emeralds of Fabienne. Her luscious lips graze mine, pulling me into a whirlwind of unexpected emotions. Together, we begin a new life, one I never imagined could exist.
    Years later, I found myself living in Rome again, never expecting to meet someone like her—an essence so pure, so radiant. I had resigned myself to the belief that love was no longer within my reach, but Fabienne rekindled flames I thought had long been extinguished. I find myself loving her with an intensity I had never known, cherishing each moment by her side as a precious treasure.
    Every glance exchanged is an invitation to dive deeper into the depths of the soul; every touch is a caress that awakens dormant senses. With Fabienne, I discover an endless palette of emotions, waves of passion

crashing over me, enveloping me in an ocean of boundless love.

In this new life we are building together, I feel enchanted, spellbound by the magic of our connection and the promise of a future where each day is an adventure we face as one. With her, I am carried into a state of delightful trance where time seems to stand still, and only the vibrant present matters, pulsing to the rhythm of our synchronized hearts.

Despite being much younger than me, Fabienne possesses a wisdom that far surpasses her apparent years. She exudes a mystical aura, akin to that of an ancient sage, with eyes that reflect the mysteries of eons past and the secrets of the universe.

In her presence, I feel transported to another time—a time when essential truths were etched into the stars and whispered by ancient winds.

As you read these words, perhaps you feel a growing warmth in your heart, a familiar sensation of connection and empathy. Perhaps, like me, you have experienced this profound, unconditional love—this instinctive understanding that transcends words and boundaries. Yet it's possible that our emotions are not entirely rooted in our own experiences, or at least not directly.

In truth, we may be absorbing the emotions of others, a phenomenon often observed in Indigo adults. These individuals, endowed with extraordinary sensitivity, can perceive and feel the emotions of those around them, often without realizing it. This gift of deep and intuitive empathy makes them particularly attuned to the emotional states of others, allowing them to understand and share feelings that may not necessarily be their own.

Indigos are like emotional sponges, constantly absorbing and reflecting the emotions of those around them. Their unique sensitivity allows them to understand, with extraordinary precision, what others are feeling. However, if not managed correctly, this sensitivity can lead to pain and confusion.

We live in a world saturated with negativity. Television, social interactions, and society itself often seem intent on spreading emotions such as hatred, loneliness, and envy. Social media only amplifies this phenomenon.

For Indigo adults, their heightened sensitivity is one of their greatest challenges. While it allows them to be deeply empathetic and compassionate, it also exposes them to emotional overload if they don't learn how to channel and protect themselves. Developing awareness of this sensitivity is crucial to turning it into a valuable resource rather than a source of suffering.

Super empathy refers to a heightened sensitivity to others' emotions. Often associated with Indigos, it describes individuals with extraordinary intuition and a deep understanding of the emotions and thoughts of those around them. Whether at work, among friends, or with family, you're constantly surrounded by others' emotions. Negative feelings—such as anxiety, anger, frustration, or depression—can be intensely felt by those with heightened sensitivity, almost as if you're "absorbing" them like a sponge. This can lead to emotional exhaustion and inner turmoil.

Emotions, like thoughts, are a form of energy. Without realizing it, you may "absorb" these energies, letting them influence your mood and state of mind. If you're prone to taking on others' emotions, it's essential to learn how to shield yourself from negative influences and redirect this energy to preserve your well-being.

When surrounded by stress or negativity, the natural defenses of sensitive individuals can erode. This drains their energy levels, aligning them with the suffering of others. Left unchecked, this process leads to emotional exhaustion. Recognizing this dynamic and adopting strategies to protect yourself is essential to maintain your balance and well-being.

Your thoughts and emotions shape your reality. It's vital not to let the negativity of others dictate your emotional state. Constantly striving to be "enough"—enough for friends, competent at work, attractive to a partner, or accomplished in life—can drain you emotionally and physically.

Indigos, with their deep sensitivity, have the potential to drive positive change. Yet, this same sensitivity can become overwhelming if not carefully managed. Learning to set emotional boundaries and protect your energy is crucial for living a fulfilling life while maintaining emotional stability.

Because Indigos often absorb the emotions of others without realizing it, they may feel destabilized and disoriented. This makes it even more crucial to develop techniques and practices for self-protection. By doing so, they can center themselves, maintain balance, and transform their sensitivity into a source of strength. This enables them not only to protect their own mental and emotional health but also to bring their unique talents into the world.

Indigos are also sensitive to the "narratives" that surround them. Like anyone else—but perhaps more intensely—they absorb societal, familial, and cultural narratives that shape their perception of themselves. These stories can trap them in limiting thought patterns, making it essential to identify and release them.

The first step to breaking free from absorbing others' emotions is reconnecting with your true self. This involves shedding the layers of false identities we've unconsciously built over time. Reconnection doesn't happen solely through mental or emotional processes but through a deep, sensory awareness of existence. It requires acknowledging your presence beyond stories and understanding that these narratives are temporary mental constructs—not the absolute truth of your being.

Here are strategies to help you protect your energy and nurture your inner balance:

- ❖ **Grounding in Presence:** Focus on the pure sensation of being and mentally repeat, **"I am."** This simple practice can help dissolve absorbed emotions, allowing you to find inner balance and peace.

- ❖ **Setting Clear Boundaries:** Establish emotional boundaries with those around you. Learn to say no and recognize when you're taking on emotions that aren't yours. Protecting your emotional space is vital to preserving your well-being.

- ❖ **Daily Energy Clearing:** Develop practices to cleanse your energy, such as meditation, spending time in nature, or even visualizing a protective barrier around you that filters out negativity.

- ❖ **Mindful Awareness:** Train yourself to identify when you're absorbing emotions that don't belong to you. By becoming aware of this process, you can choose to let go of external influences and focus on your authentic feelings.

- ❖ **Rewrite Limiting Narratives:** Reflect on the stories you've internalized from your environment. Are they truly aligned with your essence, or do they restrict your growth? Rewriting these narratives is an empowering way to align your life with your authentic self.

Indigos must learn to distinguish between their own emotions and those absorbed from the world around them. By cultivating this awareness, they can better manage their sensitivity and use their empathy constructively without becoming overwhelmed. This approach allows them to maintain emotional equilibrium while continuing to evolve spiritually and contribute positively to the world.

Remember, preserving your inner balance is essential for leading a fulfilling life. Focus on practices that reconnect you with your true self, and let this authenticity guide you in creating a life full of meaning, joy, and harmony:

### 1. Take Full Responsibility for Your Thoughts and Emotions

At times, you may feel emotions such as anger, fear, anxiety, or stress that don't seem to belong to you—almost as if they are someone else's. As a sensitive person, you have the ability to absorb these emotions, feeling them physically in your body, and they may even manifest as physical pain. This can happen not only with those closest to you—friends, family, or colleagues—but also with strangers you encounter in daily life. This hypersensitivity can quickly deplete your energy, leaving you drained and overwhelmed.

It is crucial to take full responsibility for your thoughts and emotions. What you feel is entirely your responsibility. This doesn't mean you're at the mercy of your circumstances or the emotions of others—no one has power over you unless you allow it. By acknowledging this, you realize that your emotional state is shaped by how you interpret and respond to what happens around you. Your thoughts and expectations shape the reality you experience.

When you accept this responsibility, you reconnect with yourself on a deeper level, empowering yourself to become the best version of who you are. This awareness allows you to choose how to respond emotionally and to adopt behaviors that support your well-being. In other words, you regain control over your emotional state and energy.

To strengthen this practice, avoid toxic environments whenever possible. Distance yourself from people and situations that drain your energy and leave you emotionally exhausted. Surround yourself with positive, kind, and supportive individuals. Healthy relationships nurture your spirit and help you maintain emotional balance, creating the ideal conditions for personal and spiritual growth.

Finally, remember that your sensitivity is a strength. By taking responsibility for your thoughts and emotions, you transform this sensitivity into a powerful ally—not only protecting yourself but also inspiring and supporting others.

## 2. Express Yourself Fully

Expressing yourself without fear is essential. Too often, you may find yourself in situations where someone speaks at length, and even though you'd like to contribute, you choose to remain silent for fear of seeming impolite. This silence turns you into a sponge, passively absorbing the other person's energy, which can quickly drain you and leave you feeling frustrated.

This dynamic can feel even heavier in the workplace, where colleagues or superiors might make statements you disagree with. However, out of fear of breaking professional norms or avoiding conflict, you may choose not to respond or share your perspective. This leads to a buildup of unexpressed emotions, creating inner discomfort and a sense of repression.

Many people grow up believing that their emotions and opinions are unimportant, a message reinforced by societal norms. We're often taught to follow what our parents or society expect of us, with the promise of rewards for compliance. However, acting this way means neglecting yourself, denying your authenticity, and ultimately preventing you from feeling at ease with who you truly are.

Expressing your thoughts and emotions fully is a critical step toward authenticity and well-being. When you start to speak your truth—even if it means taking risks—you become more transparent and genuine. You no longer hide behind others' expectations but dare to assert your own truth. By doing so, you reduce your anxiety because you're no longer in conflict with yourself, and you begin living as the most authentic version of you.

When you express yourself unapologetically, you respect your own needs and build more honest and meaningful relationships with others. You create a life that reflects who you truly are—without masks or forced compromises—and discover the freedom to fully realize your potential.

## 3. Be Mindful of Who You Let into Your Life

No one can enter your mind without your permission. Whether consciously or unconsciously, you invite people into your life. Every morning when you wake up, you have a certain reserve of energy. Throughout the day, this energy is spent interacting with people and handling the situations around you. Over time, this reserve depletes, leaving you tired and drained.

Some people you interact with return energy to you, creating a balanced exchange. Others, however, completely drain you. American psychiatrist Judith Orloff refers to these individuals as "energy vampires." These could be colleagues, friends, or even family members—people who draw from your energy for their benefit, leaving you exhausted and depleted.

The first step to protecting yourself is identifying such individuals in your life. Once you recognize these "energy vampires," you can become more aware of their influence and, when possible, limit or avoid contact with them. Remember, you are under no obligation to tolerate people who bring you down. You have no reason to feel guilty for stepping away from someone to safeguard your well-being.

Protecting your energy is essential to maintaining your balance and vitality. Regularly dedicate time to regenerate and center yourself. Practice meditation, yoga, spend time in nature, or engage in activities that help recharge your energy and strengthen your emotional resilience. These practices not only shield you from negative influences but also foster lasting inner peace.

Being selective about who you allow into your life enables you to create a healthy, supportive environment for personal growth. Surround yourself with people who uplift you, share your energy positively, and contribute to your well-being. By doing so, you'll be better equipped to face life's challenges and remain aligned with your true self.

## 4. You Are Not Responsible for Others

It's crucial to understand that you are responsible only for your own happiness and inner peace. To protect yourself from the negative energy of others, start by deeply loving and respecting yourself. Learning to say "no" is an act of kindness toward yourself—a way to establish clear boundaries and preserve your energy.

Remember, you have no control over how others react, act, or feel about you. Their emotions and behaviors are not your responsibility, and it's important to free yourself from this burden. Carrying the weight of others' problems and emotions only drains you and distances you from your own well-being.

When you give someone your full attention—whether they emit positive or negative energy—you transfer a portion of your energy to them. This precious energy, vital to your balance, must be managed with care. Your energy flows to what you focus on. Constantly focusing on the needs or emotions of others risks depleting you, leaving little left for yourself.

It's essential, therefore, to cultivate healthy detachment. This doesn't mean being indifferent or insensitive, but rather recognizing the limits of your responsibility. You can be present for others, support and listen to them, but without allowing yourself to be overwhelmed by their problems or emotions. Your emotional well-being must remain a priority.

To reinforce this practice, create self-care rituals that help you reconnect to your center and replenish your energy. This might include meditation, positive visualization, walks in nature, or any activity that aligns you with peace and balance. By focusing on what nourishes your mind and body, you'll strengthen your ability to say "no" without guilt and maintain healthy boundaries in your relationships.

Ultimately, freeing yourself from the sense of responsibility for others creates space to focus on your personal growth and live a more balanced, authentic life.

## 5. You Don't Need to Please Everyone

At some point, you'll realize that not everyone in your personal or professional life likes you. Some people might criticize you, complain about you, or even go out of their way to make your life more difficult. For highly empathetic individuals, dealing with toxic people—narcissists, chronic complainers, perpetual victims, or those who seek to control you—can be particularly draining.

It's vital to understand that you are not obligated to please these people. Trying to gain their approval only makes you dependent on their opinions, forcing you to sacrifice your freedom. You don't need their validation to feel good about yourself. When you learn to fully love and trust yourself, you begin to value yourself independently. At this point, you can act with confidence, stay focused on your goals, and find peace with your choices—even without the approval of others—because you're aligned with what you do and love.

Establishing clear boundaries is a key step in protecting your well-being. Learn to shield yourself from others' expectations and emotions. Set emotional limits that allow you to protect yourself, even if this means temporarily stepping away from a situation or a person. By creating these boundaries, you build a safe space for yourself where you can continue to grow without being hindered by the judgments or criticisms of others.

Remember, your well-being and fulfillment do not depend on the opinions of others. By staying true to yourself, you strengthen your autonomy and personal power, freeing yourself from the constant need to please or satisfy everyone. Your worth does not diminish because someone else fails to recognize it. When you choose to appreciate yourself, you become immune to manipulation or attempts to control you, asserting your presence in the world with strength and authenticity.

## 6. Discover the Areas Within Yourself That Need Attention

It is essential to focus on the aspects of yourself that require growth and care. When someone hurts you, what's really happening? Often, your reaction may feel disproportionate because the person acts as a trigger for unresolved issues you carry within. While they may not be directly responsible for your discomfort, they highlight the internal conflicts you're experiencing.

One key to stop absorbing other people's energy is to acknowledge and address these inner challenges. This requires deep self-exploration to identify unresolved issues and take steps to work through them. Although this process can be challenging, it is vital for your well-being and personal growth.

Take time to connect with your emotions, exploring what you truly feel and need. When you tune into your feelings, you'll become better at distinguishing your emotions from those of others. This clarity allows you to stop reacting impulsively or disproportionately to triggering situations. Instead, you'll approach these moments with balance and calm.

Working on yourself not only helps you identify and heal your emotional "weak spots," but also enables you to express yourself more authentically. By recognizing and accepting your feelings, you free yourself from reactive patterns that hold you back. You begin to act consciously from your core rather than reacting to external stimuli.

Dedicate regular time to reflect on these areas of your life. Practices like meditation, journaling, or deep conversations with a trusted person can help you uncover and address the inner conflicts that need attention. By working on these aspects, you'll strengthen your emotional resilience and become less vulnerable to external influences.

Ultimately, this journey of self-discovery is one of the best ways to avoid absorbing others' negative energies. It allows you to stay aligned with your true self, maintain emotional balance, and live a fuller, more authentic life.

## 7. Connect with People Who Remind You of Who You Truly Are

Surrounding yourself with people who help you remember your true essence is vital to avoiding negative energy and embracing positive influences. Seek the company of those who nourish you emotionally and spiritually—people who make you feel good about yourself and reinforce your sense of security and happiness.

Live with a sense of humor, smile, and don't take life too seriously Call a friend who always sees the bright side of things or spend time with a colleague who shares an inspiring and constructive perspective. These interactions help you recharge with hope and renew your confidence in yourself and your future. Optimism is contagious, and being around positive people naturally enhances your mood.

Treat yourself to simple pleasures: the foods you love, the music that moves you, or art forms that resonate with you. These activities cultivate positive emotions, fortify your inner strength, and boost your overall well-being. When you're surrounded by peace, love, and joy, you naturally thrive.

Loving and caring for yourself also increases your ability to help others. Self-love is not selfish; it's an essential foundation for giving your best to those around you.

Use compassion as a shield against invasive emotions. Compassion allows you to empathize with others without being overwhelmed by their feelings. This includes compassion for yourself. Don't feel guilty for prioritizing your well-being—it's a necessary act for growth and flourishing.

## 8. Practice Mindfulness

Mindfulness is the practice of living fully in the present moment, observing thoughts and emotions without judgment. Cultivating mindfulness helps you recognize when you're absorbing others' emotions and detach from them, enabling you to maintain inner balance and calm.

Here are some practical exercises to develop mindfulness:

### ❖ Daily Meditation

Dedicate a few minutes each day to meditation. Sit in a quiet place, close your eyes, and focus on your breath. Observe each inhalation and exhalation. If thoughts arise, acknowledge them without judgment and gently return your attention to your breath. This simple practice calms the mind and anchors you to the present moment.

### ❖ Mindfulness in Motion

Integrate mindfulness into everyday activities like walking, cooking, or showering. Pay attention to each movement, sensation, and breath as you perform these tasks. For instance, while walking, focus on the feel of your feet on the ground, the air on your skin, and the sounds around you. This helps you stay connected to the present, even during routine actions.

### ❖ Observing Thoughts and Emotions

Take time to check in with your mental and emotional state. Observe your thoughts and feelings without judging or trying to change them. If you notice that you're absorbing others' emotions or feeling drained, pause and focus on your breath. This simple act can help you regain balance and reduce stress.

### ❖ Practicing Gratitude

Spend a few moments each day acknowledging and appreciating the positive aspects of your life. This could be a delicious meal, a shared smile, or a moment of quiet. Gratitude fosters a positive mindset, helping you focus on what truly matters and detach from negative influences.

### ❖ Visual Reminders

Place visual cues in your daily environment to remind you to practice mindfulness. It could be an inspiring note on your bathroom mirror, a spiritual symbol on your desk, or a small stone in your pocket. These reminders anchor you to the present moment, encouraging you to breathe and remain calm regardless of what's happening around you.

By regularly practicing mindfulness, you strengthen your ability to remain calm, protect your energy, and experience each moment with greater clarity and serenity. This discipline creates an inner space where you can recharge and reconnect with your true self, maintaining balance and resilience even in the face of life's challenges.

## 9. Harness the Power of Visualization

Visualization is a powerful tool to shield yourself from negative energies and maintain inner balance. Imagine yourself surrounded by a protective bubble of light that envelops you, keeping you calm and serene even in stressful situations. This bubble becomes your personal shield, repelling any unwanted external influences.

Here are some techniques to strengthen this practice:

### ❖ Strengthen Your Bubble of Light

Visualize a bubble of radiant light surrounding you, charged with positive and protective energy. Imagine this light growing brighter and more intense, deflecting any negative energy. Feel its warmth and strength, noticing how it makes you invulnerable to external influences.

### ❖ Repeat Positive Affirmations

Enhance your visualization with affirmations that reinforce your sense of protection and security. For example:

*"I am surrounded by a protective light that keeps me safe. Nothing can disturb my inner peace."*

These affirmations amplify the intention behind your visualization and help solidify your inner calm.

### ❖ Create a "Protection Ritual"

Before entering environments that might be stressful or emotionally charged, take a few moments to visualize your bubble of light. You can also imagine yourself wearing armor or carrying a shield for additional protection. This ritual serves as a mental preparation, enabling you to face challenges with greater ease and confidence.

### ❖ Practice "Protection Meditation"

Spend a few minutes each day meditating on your bubble of light, deepening your connection to it. As you meditate, focus on the feeling of safety and calm that this visualization provides. Imagine the light not only surrounding you but also filling every cell of your body, nourishing you with peace and protection.

### ❖ Create a Safe Space

Designate a corner of your home as a sanctuary of peace and safety. This can be a place to meditate, relax, or simply enjoy moments of tranquility. Surround it with items that bring you peace, such as crystals, candles, or plants. Use this space to recharge your energy, meditate, and strengthen your visualization practice.

### ❖ Strengthen Yourself Through Positive Connections

Surround yourself with people who share your positive energy and inspire you. Spend time with those who see the good in life and approach challenges with enthusiasm. These interactions can fill you with hope and motivation, helping you maintain a positive mindset.

### ❖ Honor Your Needs and Cultivate Compassion

By respecting yourself and your needs, you reinforce your ability to respect and support others. Compassion, both for yourself and for others, acts as a shield against invasive influences. Protecting yourself is not selfish—it is a necessary act that enables you to become your best self and contribute to the well-being of those around you.

Through regular visualization and self-care practices, you can build a strong foundation of inner peace and resilience. This empowers you to navigate life's challenges while maintaining a sense of balance, harmony, and authenticity.

My new relationship with Fabienne teaches me every day that to love fully, it is essential to care for your boundaries, nurture your inner core, and recognize that only through personal integrity can true, authentic connection become possible.

In the same way, learning to stop absorbing others' emotions doesn't mean closing yourself off but rather discerning: allowing in only what nourishes your soul and letting the rest flow away, like water that leaves no trace as it slips past.

For the first time in a relationship, I savored an emotional freedom I had never known before—a freedom that Fabienne, with her light, had the power to reveal.

## 15 HOW TO DEVELOP YOUR PSYCHIC AND SPIRITUAL ABILITIES (WITHOUT FEAR)

*"The truth is within you; do not seek it elsewhere."* — Søren Kierkegaard

*"Everything in the Universe is within you. Ask all from yourself."* — Rumi

*"He who knows others is wise; he who knows himself is enlightened."* — Lao Tzu

As I walked along the lake with Fabienne, I allowed myself to be fully immersed in the present moment. The vibrant hues of the sky reflected perfectly on the crystalline surface of the water, creating a breathtaking panorama. During our stroll, we savored small fruits like raspberries and blueberries, purchased from a local farmer, relishing the simplicity and beauty that nature generously offered us.

With each step, the gentle rustling of leaves dancing in the light breeze filled my ears, composing a harmonious melody—a true symphony of nature. The warmth of the sun brushed against my skin, filling me with a profound sense of tranquility.

In Fabienne's company, every moment felt precious, something to be cherished. Each shared glance, every exchanged smile, wove a deeper bond between us, strengthening our connection. Walking hand in hand, the rest of the world seemed to fade away, leaving only the two of us and the stunning natural scenery that surrounded us.

In this serene setting, immersed in the wonders of nature and the warmth of love, I couldn't help but feel an overwhelming sense of peace and profound fulfillment. It was a moment to treasure, a memory destined to be etched into my heart forever.

As I reflected on Indigo adults and their extraordinary abilities, I found myself pondering once again. In the individuals I had observed, these exceptional talents often seemed burdened by fear rather than fully developed. This led me to ask:

**"How can Indigos nurture and fully express their talents, free of fear, as an authentic manifestation of their true selves?"**

You feel everything—every sensation resonates deeply. You perceive the vibrations of the universe as though no barriers exist between you and the external world. In truth, this "self" of yours is not separate from the rest of the universe.

We are living through a time of upheaval that has disrupted the natural flow of our planet's evolution, plunging society into a state of constant insecurity. This condition makes life especially challenging for you, as you experience everything with such extreme intensity.

It's no surprise that you might feel profound anger when faced with the injustices around you or that you find yourself needing more time to process past emotions. Navigating and processing these emotions and events in your daily life is a delicate yet necessary journey to free yourself from accumulated pain.

Your acute sensitivity can make you doubt yourself. You might wonder if you're capable of meeting not only others' expectations but also your own. Taking time for yourself—to discover and fully accept who you are—can feel like a challenge. Your emotions, always so raw and present, make you vulnerable, leaving you feeling drained or even unwell. Life's events and your relationships often seem complicated. Those around you may accuse you of overreacting or exaggerating, not understanding that for you, every emotion and experience is felt with overwhelming intensity, often leading to profound suffering. But this is completely natural for an Indigo adult.

*"How can I develop my abilities without fear?"*
*"How can I transform this sensitivity, which feels like a burden, into a strength?"*

The journey toward embracing your abilities begins with recognizing your unique nature. It's an inner voyage, leaving no room for fear, where every emotion becomes an opportunity for learning and growth. By learning to tame your emotions and use them as a guide rather than an obstacle, you can not only protect yourself but also fully express your potential.

The key lies in reconnecting with yourself, allowing time and space to integrate these experiences without judgment. Once you embrace your true essence, your psychic and spiritual abilities will naturally flourish, enabling you to navigate the complexities of the world with confidence.

You may often feel like you're "too much"—too sensitive, too anxious, too overwhelmed. You might even find yourself apologizing for things that aren't your fault. But the truth is, your sensitivity isn't a weakness—it's a strength. It allows you to perceive emotional nuances that others miss, granting you a unique capacity for empathy and a deep understanding of others' needs and emotions.

Instead of criticizing yourself for being sensitive, recognize it as a gift. Your sensitivity is a priceless treasure. It enables you to see the world with a depth and clarity that few possess. With this sensitivity, every moment can become an opportunity—provided you take the time to cultivate awareness. It's the key to unlocking infinite possibilities and guiding you toward achievements others may not even dream of.

Your intuition, closely linked to your sensitivity, is a remarkable talent. While intuition is accessible to everyone, Indigos like you develop it more deeply due to your unique receptivity. Consciousness isn't confined to a specific part of the body, such as the head; it transcends space and time. Intuition emerges from this higher dimension, accessible through a doorway in the unconscious.

This intuition allows you not only to understand others with extraordinary precision but also to offer them the support they need, often before they even realize it. Intuition is a form of deep knowledge that transcends belief and logic. It's an inner voice, often subtle, that guides you without relying on rational or analytical filters. It's direct and immediate, requiring no justification, yet it often proves to be profoundly accurate.

Your intuition may manifest in different ways: a strong feeling, a gut instinct, or even a sudden, clear thought that guides you toward the best course of action. This gift empowers you to navigate complex situations and make enlightened decisions, not only for yourself but also for those you care about.

To fully harness this gift, it's crucial to accept yourself without judgment or self-criticism. Instead of apologizing for your sensitivity, learn to value it. Treat it as an integral part of who you are—a powerful tool that, when wielded with confidence, can transform not only your life but also the lives of others.

By recognizing and cultivating your intuition, you'll better shield yourself from negative influences and use your sensitivity to spread positivity. Trust your instincts and listen to that inner voice—it reflects your most authentic wisdom. Don't shy away from challenges. It's essential not to impose limits on yourself, as your intuitive capacity can open unimaginable horizons. Aim high—not just to break free from predefined roles or situations but to transcend the boundaries imposed by society or your own perceptions.

Your intuition is the key to living a more authentic, fulfilling, and illuminated life. Deep down, you know you are here on this Earth to bring meaningful change. This certainty, this intuition, guides you toward a clearer understanding of your life's mission. You are not merely an observer in this world but an agent of transformation, carrying a mission that resonates deeply with your essence.

It's time to stop apologizing for who you are. Embrace and honor your spirited nature—that inner strength driving you to stand up for what you believe in and to work for a better world. Your life's mission isn't a vague idea or mere desire; it's a profound call to use your talents and abilities to create real, lasting change.

Don't hesitate to share your thoughts and express what makes you feel alive. Whether through a blog, a book, poetry, or storytelling, use your voice to inspire and guide others. Your experiences, vision, and sensitivity can help many people reflect, challenge the status quo, and find their own path to a more authentic and mindful life.

By sharing your journey and wisdom, you contribute to a collective awakening. Every word you speak, every idea you share, holds the power to inspire and uplift someone, somewhere. Don't wait any longer—your mission is unique and invaluable, and the world needs your light.

Take time to meditate. Spend time in nature; connect with trees, flowers, and the waters of a lake. This has a profound impact on your well-being, helping you recharge and restore your energy field. Explore the power of prayer and positive intentions, which, when combined, can create a ripple effect capable of transforming the world.

If Indigos are given the space to express their identity, if they are accepted and respected, they will reveal their best selves: deeply sensitive, affectionate, and talented individuals. However, without embarking on a path of personal discovery, they risk developing self-destructive or dysfunctional tendencies. Substance abuse, eating disorders, and self-harm often signal a misalignment in the life of an Indigo.

Indigo adults are born with a strong sense of purpose. They are spiritual warriors, deeply aware that they have something special to accomplish on this planet. From the moment of their birth, Indigos are often bombarded with negative messages that erode their self-esteem. They grow up hearing constant prohibitions such as:

"Don't do this" or "Don't do that,"
paired with phrases like
"You're stupid."

These messages inflict deep wounds, especially for an Indigo. When they feel undervalued, they tend to believe they are falling short, that they've failed their mission. This can spiral into depression, anger, neuroses, and even self-destructive behaviors.

For Indigo adults, it's essential to:

Remember your worth: Take time to acknowledge your uniqueness and the special contribution you bring to the world.

Allow yourself to be authentic: Accept yourself fully and give yourself permission to grow, thrive, and flourish.

Honor who you are: Recognize that your differences are a strength, not a weakness.

One remarkable trait of Indigos who reconnect with their true nature is the emergence of what could be called "superpowers." These abilities, extraordinary to others, are in fact natural gifts within Indigos—talents that arise when they align with their deepest essence.

These superpowers can manifest in many forms: exceptional intuition, profound empathy, healing energy, boundless creativity, or heightened sensitivity to the subtle energies of the universe. Indigos often also possess an innate ability to see through illusions, perceive hidden truths, and feel the emotions of others with striking intensity. Some examples of these superpowers include:

- ❖ **Advanced intuition:** A natural connection to deep inner knowing that allows you to understand people or situations without needing explicit, rational information.

- ❖ **Profound empathy:** The ability to absorb others' emotions as if they were your own, nurturing deep compassion.

- ❖ **Energy healing:** The capability to channel healing energy for yourself and others, through practices like Reiki, meditation, or visualization.

- ❖ **Generative creativity:** A vivid and overflowing imagination that produces innovative ideas, art, music, and unique solutions to complex problems.

- ❖ **Perception of subtle dimensions:** A heightened awareness of spiritual energies and entities, enabling a sensitivity to realities beyond the tangible world.

This list is by no means exhaustive, as the possibilities are infinite. Each Indigo can uncover unique abilities that emerge from their spiritual journey and inner openness. The only true limits are our imagination and belief in our unlimited potential.

For an Indigo, it's vital not to view these superpowers as a burden or anomaly but as precious tools to fulfill their life's mission. These abilities should be developed responsibly, respecting their potency, and putting them to use for both personal and collective evolution.

This process involves introspection and regular practice. Indigos need to learn how to channel their energy, purify their energetic space, and surround themselves with people and environments that support their growth. It's equally important to exercise discernment in how energy is used, avoiding waste or misuse.

In essence, the Indigo's journey is one of self-discovery, acceptance, and mastery of their unique abilities. It's about transforming every aspect of their being into something brighter, something more aligned with their divine essence.

Here lies the true alchemy: the art of creating a more evolved version of oneself that can bring light to the world. This process isn't just about personal improvement; it's about reflecting inner transformation outward, positively influencing people, circumstances, and energies around you.

It's the ability to transform the "lead" of daily struggles into the "gold" of awareness, courage, and love, crafting a life that not only reflects your authentic self but also inspires others to do the same.

This alchemy is, at its core, the art of living in harmony with your purpose—bringing meaning, beauty, and light to every corner of the world you touch.

## 16 INDIGO RELATIONSHIPS: BUILDING DEEP AND AUTHENTIC CONNECTIONS

*"Your task is not to seek love, but merely to seek and find all the barriers within yourself that you have built against it."* — Rumi

*"Self-love is the beginning of deep healing. Every loving thought toward yourself is another stone laid at the foundation of your happiness."* — Louise Hay

*"Inner peace begins the moment you choose not to allow another person or event to control your emotions"* — Pema Chödrön

Living in this world as an Indigo adult is already a challenge: you unintentionally absorb the emotions and energy of others, which can sometimes feel overwhelming. Now imagine what that means in a romantic relationship—everything becomes even more complex!

As an Indigo adult, you yearn for an intense and profound connection, not just on a physical level but also mentally and spiritually. For you, a relationship is never superficial; it's a true energetic union, a sacred space where you and your partner grow together, support one another, and elevate each other. You understand that "the whole is greater than the sum of its parts," which is why choosing your companion for this journey with care is so crucial.

It's essential to take the time to cleanse your energy and heal your emotional wounds, as these could hinder you from finding a partner who truly aligns with your essence. Entering a relationship with someone who doesn't share a similar path of spiritual growth can make the experience more complicated and, at times, frustrating.

When you're with someone who doesn't share the same qualities or characteristics of an Indigo, you might find it difficult to fully open up,

## Are You an Indigo Adult?

to go deep, and to share your most authentic self. On the other hand, meeting the "right person" for you becomes a transcendent and mystical experience. Love with this person takes on a unique dimension, where even sexuality transforms into a spiritual experience—an expression of the fundamental energy of the universe.

Your relationship becomes a channel through which this energy flows and is redirected back into the universe, enabling you to understand yourself more deeply through this unique connection.

For Indigo adults, true love is much more than a mere romantic connection; it's a spiritual journey where every encounter offers an opportunity for mutual growth, healing, and blossoming. If you're an Indigo adult, you feel an almost physical need to merge your energy with your partner's—not only on a physical level but also mentally and spiritually. Your sensitivity and deep need for meaningful connections make you particularly vulnerable to the energies around you, which is why it's crucial to choose your life partner carefully.

The risk of being misunderstood or judged is always present, as your approach to love and relationships often differs from that of the people around you. Additionally, as an Indigo, you have a tendency to "absorb" your partner's personality traits, whether positive or negative. This common trait among Indigos can make managing relationship dynamics even more challenging.

There is no perfect solution to avoid this. Even with regular cleansing of your energy field, you cannot completely eliminate the energetic influence of your partner. This exchange happens naturally and unconsciously—you may find yourself experiencing emotions, traits, or behaviors that don't belong to you but are instead absorbed from your partner. This can be destabilizing, as you instinctively recognize these feelings or actions as foreign, yet they persist because of the energetic connection.

Awareness of this dynamic is the first step to approaching your relationships with greater balance, protecting your authenticity, and maintaining emotional well-being.

This energetic exchange isn't limited to romantic relationships but can also occur with family members. However, the bond with a romantic partner is often more intense and profound. In such relationships, it's crucial to listen to yourself and maintain a degree of emotional independence, even within a deep connection, to avoid losing yourself in the other person's energies.

Ultimately, the key is finding a delicate balance between openness to connection and preservation of your personal energy space, allowing for growth together without sacrificing your spiritual individuality.

For Indigo adults, the most challenging aspect of relationships is often the spiritual connection. If your partner is not spiritually open, you may feel blocked or stifled, which can be highly unpleasant. In the short term, such a relationship might work, though you may frequently somatize this discomfort, experiencing symptoms like headaches caused by the lack of connection. However, in the long term, you may feel that something is missing, that your level of awareness has stagnated, and that you are no longer evolving. This sense of being stuck can become profoundly frustrating.

It's possible, however, that your presence could inadvertently inspire your partner to open up spiritually. Intrigued by your sensitivity, they might begin exploring the invisible and spiritual aspects of life. Conversely, if you're in a relationship with another Indigo adult, your vibrations are likely to align naturally, leading to an energetic fusion. While this deep connection can be exhilarating, it also presents challenges: for instance, if your Indigo partner has a bad day or is in a negative mood, you might absorb this energy without understanding why, regardless of your location or activity.

This phenomenon can be destabilizing unless your partner is skilled at re-centering themselves and managing their emotions positively. Moreover, as an Indigo, you might remain energetically connected to past partners even after the relationship ends. You may clearly sense when an ex is thinking of you or even feel what they are going through, as if you're still linked within a shared energetic bubble.

One critical consideration is avoiding partners prone to obsessive behaviors, as such relationships can quickly turn negative. However, being an empathetic Indigo also has extraordinary benefits: you intuitively know how to interact with your partner because you can literally sense what makes them "vibrate." If you're with another Indigo, this intuitive capacity is mutual, deepening your connection. This can make intimacy profoundly intense and fulfilling.

As an Indigo adult, choose your partners wisely. Your connection is not just physical; it's emotional and spiritual as well. These relationships can be deeply enriching but also incredibly complex.

If your partner does not share your path of spiritual growth and discovery, this can present a delicate challenge, touching the core of your personal development and search for meaning. When I first began exploring metaphysics, brain function, quantum physics, the law of attraction, and other topics that now play a significant role in my life, I found myself in an unexpected situation. My partner at the time—the person I cared about most—was not growing spiritually alongside me. This created a gap between us, making our interactions increasingly difficult.

If you're committed to spiritual growth, you are what we might call a "seeker": driven by a thirst for knowledge and inner discovery, you're willing to experiment with techniques and approaches to better understand yourself and the universe. However, if your partner does not share this quest, they may fall into the category of a "pleader." The seeker looks inward, while the pleader looks outward. Both seek fulfillment, but their approaches are vastly different.

That said, it's possible to follow different spiritual paths without it becoming a problem, provided there is mutual respect for each other's journey.

At its core, the spiritual path is a process of personal experimentation. It doesn't inherently conflict with external elements but rather focuses on an inner journey. As long as both partners are seekers, there is no conflict. However, if one is a pleader and the other a seeker, misalignment may arise, as their priorities and approaches to life diverge. The seeker is driven by a desire for understanding and growth, while the pleader may not aspire to evolve in the same way.

Spiritual development requires profound personal commitment, influencing every breath, meal, and interaction. For example, you might begin seeing food not just as nourishment but as vibrational energy composed of subatomic particles that affect your body and mind. This shift in perspective can initially be destabilizing, as it was for me, and it took me weeks to regain balance. Sharing these experiences with your partner can enrich your relationship, but if one resists or holds back, tensions may arise.

The key is allowing your spiritual maturity to translate into wisdom, understanding, and positive energy within the relationship. Keep love and acceptance at the center of your interactions, avoiding judgment and unrealistic expectations. Not everyone shares your spiritual interests, and releasing expectations will spare you much frustration. The goal is to build a relationship where each person appreciates the other for who they are without trying to change or force them into a specific philosophy.

Ultimately, we are all on a spiritual journey, whether consciously or unconsciously. It may be difficult to see this in some people's behaviors or lifestyles, but everyone seeks a better life in their own way. Spiritual awakening manifests uniquely for each individual. Avoid feeling superior or "more evolved" than your partner; remember, there was a time when you lacked the awareness you have now. True spiritual growth involves humility and grounding. If you find yourself judging your partner, ask yourself:

*"Is it truly more spiritually evolved to judge someone I love, or to accept them as they are?"*

Encourage your partner to explore new ideas or spiritual practices. This could involve meditation courses, discovering books or films on spiritual topics, or simply having open conversations about what you're learning. Every human being desires to feel alive, and if you have knowledge that could enrich your partner's life, you have a responsibility to share it. Your partner might be curious but hesitant to ask for guidance. If you maintain love and openness as the foundation of your relationship, you might be pleasantly surprised by their receptiveness.

However, it's also important to recognize when it's time to let go of a relationship that no longer works. Sometimes, despite all efforts, it becomes clear that paths must diverge. I've experienced a relationship where our worldviews grew so different that we became incompatible. Being honest with yourself allows you to recognize when it's time to move on. The risk is staying with someone out of attachment rather than true love and shared joy.

Navigating a relationship where spiritual paths differ can be challenging, but it also represents an opportunity for growth. Remember, your journey is unique, and even if your partner follows a different path, you can both learn and grow together, provided there is mutual respect.

## 17 THE TOXIC RELATIONSHIP BETWEEN INDIGO ADULTS AND NARCISSISTIC MANIPULATORS

*"Narcissists and empaths often intertwine because the narcissist seeks the unconditional love of the empath, while the empath sees the wounded soul beneath the narcissist's mask. It is a bond of illusion and dysfunction."* – Deborah Ward

*"The empath falls in love with the mask of the narcissist, not their reality. It's a toxic dance where the empath tries to heal, while the narcissist feeds on it. In this dance, the empath loses themselves, and the narcissist takes control."* – Dr. Ramani Durvasula

*"Empaths didn't come into this world to be victims; we came to be warriors. Be brave. Stay strong."* – Shannon L. Alder

Indigo adults are often seen as wise and ancient souls, endowed with an innate ability to understand others, deeply feel emotions, and perceive subtle energies. Their nature naturally drives them to heal, support, and enlighten those around them. However, this extreme sensitivity and openness to the energies of others can make them vulnerable to toxic personalities, particularly so-called "energy vampires," such as narcissistic manipulators.

A narcissistic manipulator is someone who exploits others for their own benefit without showing empathy or regard for the feelings of others. They use tactics like lying, belittling, and controlling to dominate and maintain an emotional grip on their victims, often making them doubt themselves.

Through my personal experiences with manipulative individuals, I have learned how Indigo adults can become prime targets for these destructive figures.

Energy vampires, especially narcissistic manipulators, are drawn to the inner light and generous energy of Indigos. These disturbed personalities, often plagued by deep insecurities and anxieties, desperately seek external sources to fill their internal void. They see in Indigos an endless reserve of energy, attention, and validation. This dynamic creates a toxic relationship in which the Indigo, driven by their genuine desire to help and heal, ends up being exploited and drained.

The narcissistic manipulator twists and distorts reality to reinforce their control over the Indigo. For them, the other person does not exist as an individual with their own needs and desires but must conform to the distorted vision the narcissist has of them. This type of person is arrogant, self-centered, and demands to be treated in a privileged way. They may appear charismatic, charming, and incredibly skilled at manipulating others, but they do not respect others' boundaries or accept the limits set for them.

The narcissist employs a range of tactics to maintain control, often using psychological games designed to destabilize the Indigo and make them doubt their perception of reality. They are highly critical of others and incapable of accepting dissent or criticism. When confronted with their manipulations or when their control feels threatened, they may become anxious, paranoid, or even aggressive. In extreme cases, they might lash out with uncontrollable anger when their dominance is questioned.

For the narcissistic manipulator, the Indigo represents an easy target: the more the Indigo offers love and affection, the more the narcissist feels empowered and tightens their grip. This often traps the Indigo in a toxic relationship where they are continuously belittled, humiliated, and made dependent on the narcissist's approval—a validation that will never come.

Due to their empathetic nature and innate desire to heal others, Indigos often attract wounded individuals who are desperately seeking to fill their emotional and energetic voids. However, this tendency can become a trap if the Indigo fails to establish healthy boundaries and protect their energy.

Narcissistic manipulators view Indigos as an inexhaustible resource to exploit, taking advantage of their natural inclination to forgive, understand, and give unconditionally. This makes Indigos particularly vulnerable to energy attacks and psychological abuse.

This dynamic is fueled by the illusion that the Indigo can "save" or "heal" the narcissist—an illusion reinforced by the manipulator's charisma and deceit. Driven by their sense of mission or deep compassion, the Indigo continues to give, hoping to foster positive change, without realizing they are dealing with someone incapable of receiving love in a healthy way.

The best defense for an Indigo is to sever all ties with the narcissistic manipulator. Attempts to communicate or reason with a narcissist are usually futile, as they are unlikely to change. It is essential for the Indigo to understand that this relationship cannot lead to anything constructive and that building a healthy connection with a narcissist is nearly impossible. The key lies in loving oneself enough to break free from the toxic relationship.

For Indigos, it is critical to develop an awareness of their limits and to recognize the signs of a toxic relationship early on. Surrounding oneself with like-minded individuals who can provide external perspectives and support is also helpful.

An Indigo has a choice: to remain a victim in a toxic relationship or to love themselves enough to escape the narcissist's influence. Recognizing these dynamics, understanding how they operate, and learning to protect oneself is vital to avoid repeating such patterns in the future. Indigos deserve relationships built on love, respect, and balance, and this starts with self-respect.

Protecting oneself from energy vampires does not mean stopping the act of helping others—it means learning to do so in a balanced way that preserves one's well-being. By cultivating self-love, setting clear boundaries, and applying discernment in their relationships, Indigos can continue to shine their unique light without being consumed by those who seek to extinguish it. Every relationship should be an opportunity for growth and fulfillment, not a battleground for exploitation and the erosion of self-worth.

## 18 INDIGO ADULTS: BALANCING A TRADITIONAL CAREER AND AUTHENTIC PERSONAL FULFILLMENT

*"There is no passion to be found in living below your potential."* – Nelson Mandela

*"Work is not merely a means of survival; it is a way to express who we are."* – Marc Chagall

*"True success is doing what you love and knowing it positively impacts others."* – Maya Angelou

Perhaps you've just discovered that you're an Indigo adult, or maybe you've always known, but only now are you becoming fully aware of your uniqueness.

Being an Indigo is not easy. You possess a special gift, a unique combination of talents and sensitivities, but this distinctiveness comes with its own set of challenges. If you're wondering, **'What should I do now?'** know that this book was written, in part, to provide you with the tools to answer this essential question.

In this chapter, I want to guide you through not only the difficulties that Indigos often face in traditional work environments but also the unconventional paths that may offer valuable opportunities. These alternatives can help you avoid the typical pitfalls of the professional world and allow you to fully harness your abilities in settings that honor and nurture your most authentic self.

I've already shared my difficult experience working for a large company under a manager who, to put it bluntly, turned out to be a narcissist. He even openly admitted it himself. That experience pushed me to my absolute limits.

Working for a narcissist can be emotionally devastating. Constant manipulation, a complete lack of empathy, and an insatiable need for attention and validation create a toxic work environment that breeds frustration, anger, and confusion. Such a situation can quickly become unsustainable, especially for highly sensitive individuals like Indigos.

Even without such toxic dynamics, the traditional professional landscape can be particularly challenging for Indigos in today's society.

An Indigo adult in the workplace is inherently creative and inspired, often becoming a true driver of innovation. Indigos thrive in environments that value autonomy, freedom of expression, and creativity. Thanks to their natural empathy, they can deeply understand customer needs and anticipate market trends, providing significant added value. The qualities of Indigos represent precisely what companies desperately need today: a human-centered approach to work.

Indigos should therefore be recognized and appreciated as invaluable assets in the professional world. They deserve to work in conditions that allow them to flourish fully, leveraging their natural abilities to transform business and the economy positively. Only by offering them a space where their creativity and empathy can be freely expressed can companies truly benefit from their unique potential.

Unfortunately, many corporate environments prove to be repressive, driven primarily by profit rather than purpose or ethical principles. In such structures, economic goals outweigh all other considerations, creating a particularly stifling context for sensitive and creative individuals.

This means that someone with great creativity and sharp intuition is often forced to adhere to rigid schedules (9-5), conform to strict hierarchies and structures, and navigate workplaces often plagued by unhealthy dynamics such as office gossip. In such an environment, motivation can quickly dwindle, and the invaluable spark of inspiration may be extinguished, preventing an Indigo from fully expressing their potential.

Additionally, these environments are frequently resistant to innovation, as new ideas and different approaches are often seen as threats to the established order. Those who dare to propose changes or improvements often encounter resistance, leading to frustration and isolation. It's not uncommon to attend numerous meetings devoid of real purpose, serving more to satisfy egos than to foster collective progress.

In summary, these rigid, profit-driven environments offer little room for talent development, new ideas, and innovation, making them deeply discouraging for those seeking to contribute in a meaningful and authentic way.

I have summarized the eight main obstacles that Indigos face in traditional work settings. This overview highlights the specific challenges encountered by sensitive and creative individuals in conventional and often rigid professional environments.

## 1. Discomfort with Conventions and Procedures

As an Indigo, you possess acute intuition and deep sensitivity, allowing you to grasp the bigger picture with remarkable clarity. You quickly understand the dynamics and goals of a project, making you highly effective in anticipating needs and proposing targeted solutions. This overarching vision gives you a valuable advantage, enabling you to navigate complex contexts with agility.

However, the minutiae of formal procedures, often followed more out of habit than necessity, can feel not only tedious but deeply frustrating. This bureaucratic rigidity clashes with your need for fluidity, spontaneity, and meaning, turning adherence to such conventions into a burden.

For you, administrative practices devoid of substance are more than a waste of time—they are obstacles to your ability to innovate and adapt swiftly to change. This rigid framework, constrained by inflexible rules, conflicts with your nature, which seeks harmony and purpose in every action. You thrive in environments where rules are designed to support creativity and progress, not stifle them.

## 2. Exceptional Ability to Launch Projects but Difficulty Sustaining Them

Your ability to quickly grasp the core principles of a new project or task allows you to start with energy and efficiency, often impressing colleagues and supervisors with your adaptability and sharp intuition. However, once the initial excitement fades and tasks become repetitive and predictable, your interest tends to wane.

This loss of motivation is almost inevitable because your creative and curious mind requires constant stimulation, challenges, and novelty to stay engaged and enthusiastic. For you, as an Indigo, interest and passion are not optional extras in your work; they are essential drivers that ensure the quality of your contributions. Without these elements, the daily grind can quickly feel stifling, leaving you with a profound sense of dissatisfaction and lack of purpose.

You need a delicate balance between autonomy and structure. You flourish in environments that provide the freedom to explore and create while offering clear and meaningful objectives. However, this structure should not be rigid or hierarchically imposed. Instead, it should be flexible, fostering open and fluid collaboration where ideas can flow freely and be implemented without unnecessary obstacles.

In such an innovation-driven and non-hierarchical context, you can sustain your commitment and fully express your potential. The freedom to channel your creativity, paired with sufficiently flexible guidance, allows you to focus your energy constructively and align your work with both personal and professional aspirations.

### 3. Solve Problems Creatively

You are driven by an insatiable thirst for exploration and discovery, constantly seeking new ideas to experiment with and innovative solutions to propose. You enjoy sharing your unique perspectives and collaborating with open-minded, creative individuals who fuel your desire to progress and push the boundaries of the ordinary.

However, you have a strong aversion to traditional methods and rigid structures that limit your potential and stifle your freedom of expression. To perform at your best, you need structure, but it must be flexible and adaptable, giving you the freedom to explore and pursue goals aligned with your deepest values and aspirations.

You thrive in an open, non-hierarchical environment focused on innovation and collaboration. In such a setting, your creativity has the space to flourish, and your ability to think outside the box becomes a valuable asset.

### 4. Monotony Is Your Enemy

You have a constant need for new stimuli, for projects that ignite your imagination and challenge your abilities. You flourish when faced with situations that push you beyond the ordinary, requiring invention, creation, and innovation. A dynamic work environment, where each day brings new discoveries and opportunities, is essential to keeping your enthusiasm and engagement alive.

In essence, you need a context that doesn't merely tolerate you but celebrates your uniqueness, allowing you to spread your wings and soar toward goals that hold real meaning for you and the world around you.

You find fulfilment when continuously exposed to new challenges that allow you to test your creativity. A workplace where innovation is valued and obstacles stimulate critical thinking is crucial for maintaining your interest and motivation.

Conversely, a static environment dominated by repetitive tasks and devoid of change quickly becomes unbearable. In such a setting, you experience an immediate drop in energy and a sense of suffocation that drives you to seek an escape. Your need to tackle challenges and renew yourself is a central aspect of your personality: without it, you risk losing passion for your work.

### 5. Aversion to Gossip and Manipulation

Office gossip, superficial banter, and everyday manipulations are nothing short of torture for you. Participating in such empty exchanges feels not only like a waste of time but also deeply absurd.

You have an innate need for meaningful discussions focused on constructive ideas and concrete projects—dialogues that nourish your mind and offer real value. Anything artificial or manipulative deeply unsettles you, negatively affecting your inner balance.

You are naturally drawn to authenticity, and any form of falsehood or feigned closeness erodes your professional well-being, leaving you frustrated and uneasy. To feel truly fulfilled, you need an environment that values sincerity and depth in interactions—a place where you can contribute with integrity and where every exchange serves an authentic and constructive purpose.

### 6. Desire to Challenge Senseless Rules

When faced with a rule or directive that you don't understand or that seems illogical, you find it nearly impossible to comply without feeling strong internal resistance. Your innate ability to spot inefficiencies and imagine better solutions often puts you at odds with norms you perceive as outdated, arbitrary, or unjustified.

This situation generates mounting frustration, leading you to one of two responses: withdrawing to avoid conflict or engaging in open discussions with your superiors to propose a fairer, more functional system.

You are driven by a desire for real progress based on rational logic and tangible goals, and you firmly believe there is always room for improvement. Your vision goes beyond mere rule compliance—you aspire to transform the organization to align it with principles of coherence and fairness.

## 7. Tendency to Feel Overloaded

You are naturally drawn to challenges and new opportunities, often taking on more commitments than you can realistically handle. Your passion and enthusiasm drive you to dive into numerous projects simultaneously, without always considering the impact on your time and energy.

This inclination to take on everything can lead to situations where your workload becomes overwhelming. You find yourself working harder than your colleagues, often without realizing how it happened. Over time, this pressure begins to take a toll on your balance and health, compromising your well-being and enthusiasm.

Learning to prioritize and say no when necessary is crucial for preserving your energy and maintaining your motivation.

## 8. Strong Desire to Explore New Possibilities

Your mind is constantly drawn to the endless possibilities around you, often leaping ahead to future steps long before completing what you've already started. This natural impatience, combined with your insatiable curiosity, drives you to continually seek new paths, exploring various fields and even considering entrepreneurship as an ideal space to express your creativity.

The idea of a traditional, linear, and stable career feels suffocating and uninspiring to you. You crave the freedom to explore your potential and exercise your imagination to its fullest extent. You feel a deep need to experience diverse opportunities, stay in constant motion, and uncover possibilities that fuel your curiosity, helping you grow both personally and professionally.

Indigos are agents of change. They are not simply "different" individuals; they are true spiritual warriors with a unique mission: to bring profound and meaningful transformation to our modern world. Their presence often disrupts conventions and shakes up the status quo, as they embody values and ways of living that challenge established norms.

Their existence, sometimes labeled as "alternative," is driven by an unrelenting quest for truth, authenticity, and spiritual justice. I envision a future where the extraordinary vibrational abilities and transformative potential of Indigos are fully recognized and appreciated. In that world, their energy can flow unhindered, contributing to the collective evolution of humanity.

***"But how can an Indigo adult find fulfillment in a professional environment that is often rigid and conformist?"***

Finding one's place in such a setting may seem like an insurmountable challenge, but it also presents an opportunity to reinvent the workplace according to new paradigms that resonate more deeply with your essence.

In reality, the professional world should not be seen as an obstacle but as fertile ground for those, like you, who aspire to shine while staying true to their nature.

To guide you in this pursuit of freedom and authenticity in your career, there are five fundamental strategies that every Indigo adult can apply to transform workplace difficulties into opportunities for personal and spiritual growth:

### 1. Choosing Your Profession Wisely

The Dalai Lama once said:

***"The world desperately needs more peacemakers, healers, storytellers, and people passionate about all kinds of things."***

This quote resonates deeply with Indigo adults as it reflects their most authentic mission: to use their unique abilities to bring lasting, positive change to the world.

Understanding and embracing your personal power is the first step toward finding a professional path that allows you to fulfill this mission. It is essential to choose a career that aligns with your nature—one where you can freely express your talents while making a meaningful contribution to the well-being of others and the transformation of society.

To help identify a field that suits your aspirations and abilities, here is a list of "non-traditional" professions particularly compatible with the characteristics of Indigo adults:

- ❖ **Speaker:** Share your worldview and inspire others through soul-stirring talks that awaken awareness.
- ❖ **Blogger or Vlogger:** Create content that raises awareness, provokes reflection, and encourages

change.
- **Documentary Filmmaker:** Harness the power of storytelling and visuals to uncover hidden truths and promote significant social change.
- **Inventor and Innovator:** Develop creative and groundbreaking solutions to address the challenges of the modern world.
- **Social Entrepreneur and Change-Maker:** Launch initiatives that positively transform society and generate lasting impacts.
- **Trainer or Educator:** Pass on your knowledge and skills to help others grow and thrive.
- **Coach:** Guide individuals on their journey of personal development, supporting them in reaching their full potential.
- **Therapist:** Lead others toward emotional and spiritual healing, providing them with tools for inner growth.
- **Activist or Environmentalist:** Champion causes close to your heart and work toward a more sustainable and balanced future.
- **Artist:** Express your vision of the world through creative forms such as painting, music, dance, or other visual and performing arts.
- **Author:** Write books that inspire, educate, and deeply resonate with readers, offering new perspectives and essential insights.

These professions reflect values like creativity, intuition, empathy, and the pursuit of meaning—qualities deeply rooted in the nature of Indigos. However, it's important to understand that you don't have to completely reinvent your professional life to embrace your true Indigo essence. Wherever you are right now, and whatever your career or role in the community, there is a reason you are there. Each stage of your journey has meaning and contributes to your personal and spiritual growth.

Remember, you can embody your Indigo nature in both professional and personal life without needing to change everything overnight. Sometimes, it's enough to be authentic, let your light shine, and bring your unique touch to the environment you work in. Being an Indigo is, above all, a mindset, a way of living and seeing the world. It doesn't necessarily require a radical career or lifestyle change but instead involves bringing your energy, wisdom, and sensitivity into every interaction, task, and relationship.

By staying true to yourself, you can positively transform your workplace and community, no matter your current situation. You have the ability to sow the seeds of change right where you are, simply by being yourself.

So, as you explore these "non-conventional" careers that might resonate with you, don't forget that your Indigo mission begins here and now, wherever you are. Every day offers you a new opportunity to live your truth, embody your values, and make a unique contribution to the world around you. There is no need to reinvent everything to become a fulfilled Indigo; simply live fully, with awareness and integrity, right where you are.

## 2. Taking Time to Connect with Your "Inner Essence"

Indigo adults often feel a profound responsibility when facing the challenges and problems of daily life. Motivated by an intense desire to transform and improve the world around them, they see themselves as being on a mission of change and healing. However, this mission requires significant energy, perseverance, and discernment. That's why it's essential to take the time to explore and understand your energy flow so you can use it effectively and constructively.

Learning to master your energy is crucial to becoming a true agent of change. This involves recognizing your limits, identifying sources that recharge or drain your energy, and finding ways to recenter yourself during moments of misalignment or fatigue. By cultivating this inner awareness, you can protect your well-being while staying aligned with your life's mission.

Remember, your role as an Indigo adult is not only to solve problems but also to serve as a beacon of light and transformation for those around you. By balancing your energy, you can positively influence others, foster lasting change, and contribute authentically to the collective awakening.

## 3. Advancing in the Discovery of Your "Life Mission"

As previously mentioned, Indigos possess extraordinary sensitivity and intuition that distinguish them from a young age. Their purpose is to awaken consciousness and guide the way toward a more harmonious and sustainable world, prioritizing collective well-being and balance.

Discovering and fully understanding your life mission is an evolutionary process, closely tied to your personal growth journey. This mission might not reveal itself immediately or in its entirety, and it's normal not to grasp its full profile right away. Every step of your path, every experience, and every challenge brings you closer to understanding your purpose. It is a journey that requires patience and trust, as only by advancing step by step will you connect more deeply with the energy driving you forward.

It is important to remember that even if you do not yet have a clear vision of your mission, every action you take brings you closer to that sense of inner alignment. The journey toward your life mission is just as significant as the mission itself, as it equips you with the strength, wisdom, and tools necessary to fulfill your purpose.

If you encounter moments of doubt or discouragement, know that these phases are also part of your journey. They offer opportunities to reflect, recenter yourself, and strengthen your resolve. Remember, your life mission is not something to uncover all at once but rather a journey that unfolds over time, with stages that reveal themselves gradually. Embrace this journey with curiosity and an open mind, knowing that every moment, encounter, and decision guides you closer to your inner truth.

## 4. Learning to Use New Tools

To navigate this world without being overwhelmed by negative energies, you need tools to help you manage your environment. It is essential to learn how not to unconsciously absorb the emotional burdens around you, preventing feelings of exhaustion or alienation in a world that often feels foreign to you.

Practices such as daily meditation, visualizing energetic

protection, or grounding can help you maintain your inner balance. Similarly, learning to recognize and establish healthy boundaries with others is crucial for preserving your energy and approaching daily interactions with calm and strength.

## 5. Healing Your Emotional Wounds

To heal the world, you must first begin by healing your emotional wounds. As an Indigo, the depth of your life experiences requires an approach that goes beyond traditional psychological methods. You need to embark on a deeper and more spiritual journey, allowing you to address the roots of your suffering and blockages, transforming them into opportunities for growth and change.

There are many paths to initiate this essential healing work. These include spiritual practices such as meditation, visualization, energy work, or connecting with nature. Other paths may involve alternative therapies like hypnosis, emotional release techniques, or cellular memory healing. Whatever method you choose, it is important to approach it with intention and openness, giving yourself the time needed to explore and transform the deepest parts of your being.

Healing also means letting go of the need to conform to others' expectations. Too often, we lose ourselves in trying to fit into external norms and judgments, forgetting our true nature and most authentic desires. Remember that your thoughts and words have immense power to shape your reality. By becoming aware of this power, you can start making choices that truly reflect who you are.

Learn to recognize the connections between the events in your life, to notice synchronicities and the signs the universe sends you. Strive to understand the hidden meaning behind every experience, whether positive or negative, and use these lessons to grow and evolve. Stay aligned with your body, mind, and soul. By being true to yourself, listening to your intuition, and respecting your own rhythm, you will find the path to a life that is more authentic, fulfilling, and in harmony with your true essence.

The famous text "Here's to the Crazy Ones" is an Apple advertisement launched in 1997, and I believe it perfectly illustrates what

I aimed to convey in this chapter. The words of this ad deeply resonate with the idea of not conforming to others' expectations, following your own path, and having the courage to be authentic, even when it feels difficult or radical.

You can easily find the narrated version of the text online. I encourage you to watch or listen to it, as I am convinced it will resonate deeply with you, just as it did with me. It embodies an essential message: dare to be different, dare to be yourself, and, in doing so, dare to change the world.

Below is the text:

*"Here's to the crazy ones.*
*The misfits. The rebels. The troublemakers.*
*The round pegs in the square holes.*
*The ones who see things differently.*
*They're not fond of rules.*
*And they have no respect for the status quo.*
*You can quote them, disagree with them, glorify or vilify them.*
*But the only thing you can't do is ignore them.*
*Because they change things.*
*They push the human race forward.*
*And while some may see them as the crazy ones, we see genius.*
*Because the people who are crazy enough to think they can change the world,*
*are the ones who do."*

# 19 HOW TO HELP AN INDIGO ADULT

*"Go confidently in the direction of your dreams. Live the life you have imagined."* - Henry David Thoreau

*"Do not be satisfied with the stories of how things have gone for others. Unfold your own myth."* - Rumi

*"Be the change you wish to see in the world."* - Mahatma Gandhi

Perhaps you are not an Indigo yourself but believe someone close to you is, and you wish to connect with this person or perhaps help them. Or maybe you are an Indigo looking to support other Indigos in their growth journey.

In this chapter, I share some insights on how to do so, based on my direct experience.

Indigo adults face a significant challenge: despite possessing rare, even extraordinary abilities, they must learn to balance their inner being with the outer world. They do not feel they are in their "true" home, and the rules of this world often feel unfamiliar or alien. Although they carry within them an unconditional love, they live in an environment where this love is not always reciprocated or understood.

If they are ready to harness their "superpowers"—their strong intuition, deep empathy, and subtle perceptions—it is crucial that their actions align with the purpose they have set for themselves in this life. This does not mean scattering their energy, wasting their generosity, or being swept away by illusions, whether in love or other areas. It would be like "casting pearls before swine," wearing an elegant suit to wash a car, or squandering a fortune by giving indiscriminately to anyone.

Indigos must learn to discern what deserves their effort and what does not, to preserve their resources, and to act with awareness, ensuring that their energies are not wasted but instead contribute to their growth and that of others.

Indigos must develop a profound sense of responsibility toward themselves. This is a sign of maturity and personal evolution. Taking on this responsibility means knowing when and how to use their abilities, avoiding their dissipation in self-destructive or unproductive dynamics. It is vital that an Indigo recognizes the value of their abilities and learns to apply them to situations where they can be truly appreciated and make a positive contribution.

A crucial aspect to consider is the inadequacy of today's society in accommodating Indigos. Our society is built on principles of competition, hyper-productivity, greed, and resource scarcity, upheld by outdated beliefs and structures that no longer serve—if they ever did—the collective evolution. The dominant culture fosters isolation, constant competition, and chronic dissatisfaction, dynamics that conflict with the spiritual and sensitive nature of Indigos.

For an Indigo, passively accepting this reality is not an option. They must understand that the current society cannot fulfill their deepest needs or their spiritual mission. This does not mean completely rejecting the world but realizing they are called to create a new model—a new way of living that aligns with their values and essence. It is essential for them to recognize their capacity to positively influence the world and manifest a reality more in line with their ideals.

Indigos are destined to transcend the limitations imposed by today's society—not to settle for what is but to use their abilities to actively contribute to a world that is more just, aware, and compassionate. By practicing discernment and staying true to their authentic nature, they can navigate this world with greater clarity, strength, and serenity.

This is not about simply accepting society as it is or completely abandoning it, but rather understanding that we are part of this system and that our collective actions have created or sustained the structures of the past.

Many ask:

*"Should I continue following a societal model that no longer aligns with me?"*

Then comes another question:

*"Should I find a balance between the old world and the new?"*

And finally, the ultimate question arises:
*"Am I ready to create a new model, a new world?"*
These questions are fundamental to our evolutionary process. The path forward seems to unfold in three phases: first, rejecting the old system that no longer resonates with our deepest aspirations; then, entering a transitional phase, where we find ourselves between two worlds; and finally, actively committing to building a new model—or better yet, envisioning a world free of rigid frameworks, with structures that foster true freedom and creativity.

Instead of lamenting the current situation, we must channel all our creative energy into actively contributing to the birth of the new world we wish to see. This means strengthening ties with those who share our vision of a fairer world and allowing ourselves to fully realize our mission on this Earth.

By embracing this inner revolution and creating new structures of thought and action, we can pave the way toward a better future.

We go through distinct phases: rejecting, confronting, and finally, creating. It is in this final phase—the phase of creation—that we find the highest frequency, the greatest joy. Here lies the true power of the Indigo: to love and to create. By aligning their unconditional love with their innate desire to create, Indigos contribute not only to their own evolution but also to that of the collective.

For Indigos, it is not about adapting to a world that does not reflect their essence but about actively participating in the emergence of a world more aligned with their deepest values. Creating this new world means fully expressing their authentic nature and inspiring others to do the same.

This is the true path of the Indigo: to transform, innovate, love, and create. Each individual, based on their abilities, must learn to live by improving themselves—transforming their weaknesses into strengths, their limitations into opportunities.

This personal evolution is akin to an inner alchemy: it is about working miracles, transforming shadow into light, lead into gold. For Indigos, it means increasing the light and "spiritual gold" they carry in their hearts and rooting it firmly in this ever-changing Earth. It is not an easy task, but it is in this challenge that the beauty of their mission truly lies.

# CONCLUSION

**Boccadoro:** "Just open that door at the end to travel back or forward in time, like in a fairy tale."

**Corto Maltese:** "It would be wonderful to live in a fairy tale."

**Boccadoro:** "But you live constantly in fairy tales. When an adult enters the world of fairy tales, they can never leave again. Didn't you know that?" — From "The Golden House of Samarkand" by Hugo Pratt

*"Why is this winter morning different from all the others?"*
As the first rays of sunlight pierce through the trees, light filters through the branches along the path of an old countryside residence, creating luminous patterns on the frost and gently illuminating the sleeping landscape.

*"In truth, I suspect the only one who has changed is me, because everything here has stayed the same."*
The time had come to internalize what I had learned about Indigos, to live more consciously and find inner balance: connecting with others, with my love, with the planet.

I embark on this mission with a renewed determination. It is not an easy task, but this inner calling is irresistible. There is a sweetness in this quest, a promise of peace and wholeness that I cannot ignore.

Morning meditation. Sitting silently, eyes closed, letting my mind settle. This practice helps me bring hidden emotions to the surface, observe them without judgment, and accept them as part of myself. It is a beginning. These moments of stillness and motion are starting to transform my life.

I treat my body with greater respect: healthy eating, regular exercise. My emotional and psychological well-being is improving. I feel calmer, more at peace. This inner serenity changes how I perceive the world and human relationships.

Joining discussion and sharing groups. Finding kindred spirits, ready to explore their inner paths. These exchanges are rich and nourishing. Everyone brings their wisdom and vulnerability.

Spending more time immersed in nature. The beauty of forests, rivers, and mountains reminds me of my connection to the Earth.

Loving myself allows me to offer purer, more authentic love to my partner. My ability to listen and understand others deepens. I become a more present and empathetic friend.

By caring for my personal ecology—emotions, health, psychological well-being—I find inner balance. I create deeper, more meaningful connections with others, with my love, with the planet.

This journey to oneself is an endless path. Each step brings new discoveries, new transformations. Every conscious action nourishes a life that is more harmonious and connected.

That winter morning, as the sun's rays warmed my face, I knew I was on the right path—the path to a life filled with meaning, peace, and love.

***"What are you doing out here?"*** Fabienne asked as she joined me.

***"I think I'd like to write a book, to share everything I've learned and make a bigger impact."***

The first words of this book were written that very day, in an old countryside house:

*"You are a miracle; you are your own miracle."*

I wrote this book to help you realize this truth. Each day, we overlook our own greatness, blinded by petty frustrations and endless doubts. But now is the time to look beyond those clouds that obscure our vision.

Imagine yourself in the heart of a beech forest, surrounded by majestic trees. Feel the earth beneath your feet, solid and reassuring. You are here, now, fully alive. This moment, this simple instant, is a miracle. And you are its most essential part.

Take a moment to breathe deeply. The air filling your lungs is a gift, a source of inexhaustible life. Your heart beats faithfully and steadily without requiring your attention. Every gesture, every step you take is a unique dance within the universe.

Never forget that.

I remember sitting by a lake one day, watching the sunset turn the water into a vast golden expanse. In that moment, I realized that every human being is a divine spark, a unique expression of life.

We all carry this light within us, ready to shine if we only allow it. Yet too often, we trap ourselves in mental cages built from fear and insecurity. We compare ourselves to others, judge ourselves harshly, and forget an essential truth: we are miracles, each of us.

The simple act of existing is an act of courage and beauty.

By reconnecting with yourself, you will discover a profound peace, a quiet certainty. You will face life's storms with agility and hope, understanding that every challenge is an opportunity to grow and every trial a chance to uncover a new facet of your being.

You are your own miracle. And the world needs your light, your truth, your love. Never forget that.

If you have just discovered that you are an Indigo adult, you are part of a wonderful family of souls: warriors of the spirit, artisans of light, those who bring positive change to our planet.

I understand that for some, all of this may seem like science fiction. However, as we reach the conclusion of this book, I am certain that something has resonated within you, leaving you with the sense that there is a kernel of truth you already knew.

I have a clear sense that life is simply the collection of impressions we capture in the moment we are underwater, just after a dive, before we resurface and emerge back into reality.

We have reached the end of our journey together. I hope I have offered you many impressions—ones you can carry with you, let yourself be inspired by, and use to open new doors within yourself.

**I wish you a wonderful continuation of your journey.**

If you enjoyed this book or found it meaningful, I would be truly grateful if you could take a moment to leave an honest review on Amazon. Your feedback not only helps me grow as an author but also supports other readers in discovering this work.

**Thank you for your time and kindness!**
 **Stefano Pratt**

# ABOUT THE AUTHOR

*"Every word you speak, every idea you share, has the potential to inspire and transform someone, somewhere".*

Stefano Pratt, an author, soul explorer, and visionary, embodies this philosophy through his writings. Drawing inspiration from the mysteries of the world and the depths of the human spirit, he seeks to awaken consciousness and provide answers to life's profound questions. Passionate about spirituality, psychology, and the pursuit of meaning, Stefano delves into topics such as Indigo adults, the primordial energies of nature, and pathways to personal fulfillment.

While he isn't an avid fan of social media, you can connect with him directly at stefanopratt@gmail.com.

Printed in Great Britain
by Amazon